Sri Babaji:

Immortal Yogi of the Himalayas

Sri Babaji:

Immortal Yogi of the Himalayas

ROMOLA BUTALIA

With an introduction by Sri Gorakh Babaji

Vasudeva Kutumbakam
Chief distributor: Motilal Banarsidass Publishers Pvt Ltd.

First Edition: 2007

ISBN: 978-81-208-3257-2

Vasudeva Kutumbakam
Manasarovar Kailash Kutir, Annapurna Parisar,
Gurukul Marg, Vrindavan 281121

Chief distributor:
Motilal Banarsidass Publishers Pvt Ltd., Delhi
www.mlbd.com e-mail: mlbd@vsnl.com

Printed & bound at:
Raj Press, R-3 Inderpuri, New Delhi 110 012

Also available at:
MOTILAL BANARSIDASS
Delhi: Tel (011)23851985, 23858335
Mumbai: Tel (022)23516583, 32922105
Kolkata: Tel (033)22824872, 32967029
Bangalore: Tel (080)26542591, 32711690
Chennai: Tel (044)24982315, 3290259841

About the Author

Romola Butalia did her Masters from Delhi School of Economics before establishing herself as a journalist of repute. With the advent of satelite television in India, she shifted to the visual medium, later making different kinds of films. She was one of the first to explore the potential of the Internet as a partner in India's first horizontal portal. Thereafter, she became head of portals for India's second largest multi-channel portal. She continues to be Editor of India Travelogue: www.indiatravelogue.com

Her search for Truth led to a continued tryst with the Himalayas and the blessings of many *sant-mahatmas.* Her first book, ***In the Presence of the Masters***, has been widely acclaimed. As a practitioner in the tradition of the Himalayan *yogis,* she is known as Sriji.

She can be contacted by e-mail: editor@indiatravelogue.com

ॐ

ॐ Sri Ganeshaya Namaha – Auspicious One, first to be worshipped

Thy grace removes obstacles, doubt and conflict.

ॐ Sri Maha Saraswatiye Namaha – bestower of knowledge and wisdom

Command thou my thought and speech.

ॐ Sri Brahmane Namaha – who abideth in all things

With thy blessings is attained Dharma, Arth, Kaam, Moksha.

ॐ Sri Maha Lakshmiye Namaha – Goddess of fortune and well-being

Giver of all that is munificent and good.

ॐ Sri Vishnave Namaha – all-pervading

Thou taketh form to restore Dharma in every age

And remaineth as Narayana, adored by saint and sage.

ॐ Sri Maha Kaliye Namaha – dread of the dreadful, fear of the fearless

Conqueror of Death, Beloved of Shiva

Thy forms are many: terrifying and benevolent

Ya Devi: tapaswini, yogini, Param Shakti Mayi

Great yogis have fallen short in praise of thee.

ॐ Shivaya Namaha – Mahayogi amongst yogis,

Avadhut of the Himalayas, Adisiddha beginningless and endless

Thy form is the sacred Kailash

Eternal abode of Bhawani-Shankar Uma-Parvati.

ॐ Sada Shivaya Namaha - at Thy Lotus Feet

Into the sacred Fire of Being, I offer the Self in Gyan-Yagya

The Fire is Brahman, the offering is Brahman, what remains is Brahman

Eternal, Perfect, Unchanging

ॐ Gurubhyo Namaha

Contents

List of Photographs

Cover photograph of Sri Gorakh Babaji courtesy Alok Johri

Photographs 1, 2, 3 & 15 courtesy Sri Gorakh Babaji

Photograph 4 courtesy Swami Parmananda Puri

Photograph 11 courtesy Alok Johri

All other photographs Romola Butalia

ॐ

Introduction

ॐ

ॐ Sri Ganeshaye Namaha
ॐ Guruve Namaha

This book has been written as a broad-based search. The writer, Romola Butalia, given the name of Sriji at the Kumbha in Ujjain, has made incalculable effort through varied and often difficult terrain, visiting many ancient sacred temples, *teerth sthans* or places of pilgrimage and *tapasya sthals* where *tapasya* or austerities have been performed. It is written from *anubhuti* or experience, with *bhav* or devotion and from the heart, while still remaining an analytical study.

Jaki rahin bhavna jaisi, Prabhu murat dekhi tin taisi

(According to our devotion will be our experience)

Direct experience is not measurable and remains inexplicable. Even at a sacred place, all will not experience the same energy. It is directly connected to the individual's vibrations and his *bhav.* For one without purity of purpose it can, at best, be a pleasurable experience; a change from his usual state of mind, nothing more. The mind that moves will continue to move. It may be stilled momentarily, but the effects will not be lasting, the memory will be merely of the pleasant, it will not have a transformational impact.

Beyond the mind and senses, some of my own experiences, which are not contained in books or in told tales, the reader is welcome to receive or discard. About *siddha-sants,* there are stories told which do not belong to the ordinary realms of consciousness. Those who find it difficult to believe these are well-advised to believe what the rational mind, in keeping with current accepted scientific knowledge, readily accepts.

The *mahima* or praise of Sri Babaji is *apaar* or beyond definition. He cannot be understood through the medium of a single name or single form. He has many forms, both *nirakar* and *shakar,* both with and without manifestation. The many forms and names by which he has been known, the different sacred *sthans* with which he is associated, the *ashrams* and *mandirs* which were consecrated by him, the various *teerth sthans* he visited, the *gufas, kutias* and *tapasya sthals* where he lived, the rivers and paths along which he walked, are the way to know him. It is the way to know the Truth sought by *karma-yogi, gyan-yogi* and *bhakti-yogi* alike.

Among the many *sant-mahatmas* of his time who were known to have held him in the highest regard are Sombari Baba, Sitaram Baba, Laturia Baba, Jangam Baba and Bagambari Baba. There were many others, both known and unknown.

Manmunindra Mahavatar Hairakhandi Babaji had spent his life in *tapasya, sadhana, japa, anusthan,* establishing and consecrating *mandirs,* in *bhraman* sharing his spiritual light everywhere he went. Each of the places where he had remained in *tapasya* and *sadhana* are a living light to his memory. His *yoga sadhana, yagya, anusthan* can be realised even today. His simplicity, the depth of his wisdom and the intensity of his *sadhana* is beyond mere words. He had reached the highest state of *siddhatwa* and of *rishittwa.* He had transcended the *panch tattwas* or five elements of *bhumi* or earth, *jal* or water, *agni* or fire, *vayu* or air, *akasha* or ether, and the *triguna* (triple attributes) of *satwa* or purity, *rajas* or action and *tamas* or inertia. He was a *trikal darshi* (one who is beyond Time, having realised the past, present and future) *atman–anubhavi* (enlightened Soul) *mahapurusha* (evolved Being) and *mahayogi* (*Yogi* among *yogis*). *Sadhus, sants* and *bhakts* of all creeds and denominations, both *sanyasins (Shaivites)* and *tyagi-vairagis* (Vaishnavites) received his blessings. He was a *nishkama karma yogi* and *Samkhya yogi.*

He had given courage to many national heroes of the time who strove for freedom through the Independence movement. He was the embodiment of *karmayoga, gyan-yoga* and *bhakti yoga* praised in the *Bhagwad Gita.* All who are on the spiritual path be they *sanyasin, vanprasthi, brahmachari* or *grihasthi,* continue to receive his silent blessings. Many of these experiences have been recorded in this book.

Baba Sri is an *amar rishi* or deathless. *Mrityuloka, swargaloka, siddhaloka, rishiloka, patal naga loka, devaloka, goloka, saket loka, Brahma Loka, Vaikutha Loka, Shiva Loka,* are all accessible to *siddhas.* These are not matters of great surprise. This is within the realm of possible for *rishis* and *siddhas.* The *shastras* or scriptures are the *praman* or proof of this.

In *mrityuloka,* Baba Sri had *kayic siddhi.* This was known to many of his devotees. Commonly known is that he was simultaneously seen at Kumaon–Kailash *gufa* beside the Gautami Ganga river near Hairakhan village; at Kurukshetra; and at Haridwar, during a particular eclipse. Those who witnessed it are no longer alive, but *janashruti* or folklore and accounts in books, carry this legend forward. At another time, near Karanprayag en route to Badrinath, the *antim samskara* or final rites of his lifeless body was completed, while at the same time, devotees bear witness to the fact that he never left the *gufa* of Kumaon Kailash.

It is impossible to describe or mention all the places that Babaji had been in his lifetime of *bhraman.* The ones mentioned are those which the writer has visited and had first hand experience of. In the current context, this book is limited primarily to Kumaon. This is the region of Kurma or Kacchyap *avatar* of Lord Vishnu when the *samudra manthan* or churning of the oceans by the *devas* or gods and the *danavas* or demons occurred. Also mentioned are some places in Garhwal, regarded as the land of Narasimha *avatar.* Kumaon is the land of *Shakti:* it is the land of Mata Sati, the fountainhead of the 52 *shaktipeeths.* It is where Parvati Mata, the embodiment of perfection, manifested.

Before knowing the various places in Uttarakhand Himalayas with which Sri Babaji is associated, it is imperative to remember that he had travelled widely in Himachal, Jammu-Kashmir, Sikkim and throughout the Himalayas. It is almost impossible to write his history because there are no records, and much has been lost over time. *Jeta jana teta bakhana* (as much as is known can be described). His history is believed to span two centuries from the middle of the 18th century to the first quarter of the 20th century.

Sri Babaji is known to have undertaken numerous journeys to the various *dhams* and *teerth sthans.* He is known to have visited the Sri Ram *shaktipeeth* at Ayodhya, and the Radha-Krishna *shaktipeeth* at Braj Dham.

His wide travels include Kailash-Manasarovar, when he stayed at all the places en route through India, Nepal, Tibet as well as on the *parikrama marg* of both Manasarovar and Kailash. At many places, he stayed in *kutias* as also *gufas* or caves and even *jal gufas* or underwater caves, where he had stayed in his *siddhatwa swarup.* In the 3 day *parikrama,* which is still open to pilgrims, Baba Sri had done *sadhana.* He had also done *tapasya* along the longer *parikramas* of one month, three months and six months, which are no longer accessible. At Manasarovar, there used to be a *sadhu Kumbha,* when *sadhus* would bathe in the Manasarovar, specially during *Guru Purnima.* In this region, *siddhas* have taken *jeevit jal samadhi.* Other *sadhus* in *bhav,* have given up their bodies here. Still others, who lived essentially in their physical bodies, were blessed to breathe their last here, overcome by the cold and the difficulties of the journey.

In Nepal, beside the river Bagmati, is the famous Pashupatinath temple and the Guru Gorakhnath *dhuna* at Mrigsthali. Baba Sri had visited the villages and *gufas* alongside the Narayani and the Gandak rivers, as well as the *siddha sthans* on mountain-peaks. The Nepal royal family also knew him well. *Sadhus* from different *sampradayas* would visit Pashupatinath en route to Kailash. Baba Sri had been acknowledged by the royal family as the *sangrakshak* or protector of this *yatra.* The *tapasya sthals* of Shiva-Gorakshanath, Sri Matsyendranath and other *rishi-munis* were familiar to Baba Sri who had done *tapasya* in them.

He was known as Nepali Baba and Lama Baba in Nepal and Tibet. Another name, by which he was known among evolved *Hamsas* and *Paramhamsas,* was Paramhamsa Hairakhandeshwarananda Yati. In this *rup* or form he is among the *siddha yatis,* who live in their *avadhut* aspect.

In Tibet's Nyalam, Khasa, Shigatse, Lhasa and other places, Baba Sri had done *ugra tapasya* in *kutias* and *gufas.* He had also been through China as Lama Baba. From Kashmir's Pamir through Suleman Parvat, Hindu Kush and onto Medina Mecca, he had done *bhraman* as a *sufi* saint. As a *siddha yogi,* he can do *bhraman* in any *rup* or form. Sitaram Baba, who is over 110 years, and lives at Bridh Jageshwar, also states this.

The Himalayas are the land of *deva-devis,* of *rishi-munis,* of *siddhas,* of *avatars* and of *yogis* and saints. Uttarakhand has been called *devabhumi* because of this. The many rivers that flow here, as well as the many rivulets that flow into them, are all regarded as sacred. These flow through the plains thereafter. Water is integral to life, and it is said, *Jale Vishnu, Thale Vishnu* or the water is Vishnu, the earth is Vishnu. Some major rivers that are important from the religious as well as environmental perspective are Bhagirathi-Ganga from Gangotri, Yamuna from Yumnotri, Alakananda from Badrinath and Mandakini from Kedarnath, as well as Saryu, Sarda, Gomati, Panaar, Padmavati, Kheer Ganga, Barhai Ganga, Rama Ganga, Koteshwari, Ghatgarh, Airi Ganga, Kosi, Kshipra, Dhauli Ganga, Kali Ganga. All are aspects of the sacred Ganga.

The *tapasya sthals* and *siddha sthans* of *rishi-munis* and *siddhas* are oftentimes beside these sacred rivers, at the congruence of rivers, or on mountain peaks. The Himalayan mountains are truly divine, created by the Supreme Being for the gods.

It is important to mention the primary places of spiritual significance. I have lived and done *sadhana* and *tapasya* at innumerable *siddha sthans* and at the *sangam* of rivers, to recognise the spiritual and divine energies associated with them. I have practised austerities, taken ritual bath, kept fast, done *tapasya,* maintained *anusthan, sadhana* including *dhuna-sadhana, naam-japa, yantra-sadhana, yoga, dhyana, kirtan, bhajan,* through *tyaga* and *vairagya* or renunciation, at each of these places. This was to invoke divine energies, for the blessings of the *rishi-munis* and gods-goddesses and to have direct experience of the various methods of worship and of invoking energies that have come to us through *parampara* or tradition. Through sacred worship at these *siddha sthans* and *tapasya sthals,* it is possible to glimpse these Eternal Truths and eventually, to realise the Absolute.

There are sacred energies associated with different places. Where these energies have been invoked in the past, where the Highest Truths have been revealed, where *rishi-munis, siddhas* and *yogis* have done *sadhana* and *tapasya,* these energies remain dormant and can be invoked through purity of worship and through total renunciation. These remain eternally present in subtle form. To realise these, one must transcend the physical and be in the spiritual realms and dimensions of sacred energies. In current times, many places of worship, including temples and religious *teerth sthans* have become polluted because of the *rajasic* and *tamasic* activities that now abound there. Those with purity of vision, purity of heart, purity of mind, should continue to stay in these places so that the energies remain manifest, else the external form hides the divinity of the sacred places.

This book is about these sacred places and events. They provide a glimpse of the path of *gyan-yoga, karma-yoga, bhakti-yoga, prem-yoga* and *tapasya-yoga.* It is of importance to those who tread this path. There are places mentioned of which there is little or no knowledge. Of special significance are the many recorded meetings as told by those individuals, both *sants* and *bhakts,* who had Baba Sri's *darshan* or blessings, mostly in their childhood. Many families, individuals and *sant-mahatmas* with whom Baba Sri maintained habitual contact were visited. The writer undertook this journey through *sadhana, yagya, naam-jap,* with *bhav* and purity of heart and action.

The Himalayas are the very source, they are the form of Narayana Himself. Lord Krishna had said in 10.25 of the *Gita,* "Among the *sthir* or constant, unmoving, I am Himalaya." Saints are the beloved of Narayana, the *nitya avatar* of Narayana. Himalayan *tapaswi yogis* are connected to that source. It has been the tradition in the Himalayas, that when householders maintain *tapasya,* they are regarded as equivalent to a *sanyasin.*

Sri Hairakhandi Babaji's *darshan* is of *satya* or truth, *saralta* or simplicity and *prem* or love. His practical philosophy of simple living and high thinking, and of universality, is the basis of peaceful co-existence and true progress. *Sanatan Dharma* is a religion of *anusthan* or worship, not of *prachar* or preaching. His words were few, simple and direct. He inspired people by his actions and his behaviour, he did not resort to oratory. He worked towards the spiritual upliftment of all who came in contact with him. Many of the political leaders of the time were influenced by him. He has inspired and influenced innumerable *yogis* and *sant mahatmas* of the time, and he continues to do so through the power of his thought vibrations. His *yoga bal* still has the power to inspire *sant mahatmas* and sincere seekers.

HIMALAYAN YOGI SRI GORAKH BABAJI

Siddha Darshan

Sri Manmunindra Mahavatar Hairakhandi Babaji

Hairakhan Babaji
sometimes referred to as Bramhachari Baba

CHAPTER 1

Sri Babaji

ॐ

Twameva Mata cha Pita Twameva
Twameva Bandhu cha Sakha Twameva
Twameva Vidya Dravinam Twameva
Twameva Sarvam Mama Deva Deva

— *Shloka/Prayer*

Thou art my mother and my father
Thou Art my friend and my companion
Thou art Knowledge and Wealth
Thou art all that is, the ever-existent Supreme Being

The legendary Babaji is known by different names in many places through centuries of time, in what appears to be a seemingly unsolvable mystery. He has been referred to simply as 'Babaji' in most instances when he has given *'darshan'*. He belongs in the realms of the *rishis, siddhas* and *yogis,* the sages and the masters. He moves in different *lokas* or realms, different times and spaces. Babaji is deeply revered and loved by those whose lives have been touched by his *darshan.* He moves with utmost simplicity among his devotees, his disciples and those who seek his presence with an open heart. To them he has revealed some of his many faces.

He has been described as wearing a *juneau (Brahma sutra)* or sacred thread, referred to as Brahmachari Baba and connected to Lord Brahma. Others have connected him to Narayana, the eternal master, who is an aspect of Lord Vishnu.

He has often been spoken of as Manmunindra Baba, and on occasion moved in his *avadhut* aspect, when he was associated with Lord Shiva. As a perfect *siddha*, he is related to Gorakhnath, also revered as Shiva Goraksha.

He is known as Guru Gorakhnath in Nepal; referred to as Lama Baba in Tibet, where he spent time; and Kanchopi Topa Baba in the Uttarakhand Himalayas, from the cap he habitually wore. More recently, and in some traditions of South India, he is known as Kriya Babaji, because he initiated many masters into the mysteries of *Kriya Yoga* and is known for his propagation of *sahaj samadhi.* While he has generally worked in relative anonymity there are several references to him by many different masters, presently working in the world.

Some people refer to him as Mahavatar Babaji, from Paramhamsa Yogananda-ji's book, *Autobiography of a Yogi*, which refers to Lahiri Mahashaya's meeting in 1861. Lahiri Mahashaya, who had developed yogic powers, had referred to him as Babaji. According to *Vedic Sanatan* spiritual philosophy, *Mahavatar* is the transcendental Truth, the very fountainhead revealed in form through the *avatars.* While the *Mahavatar* is supremely free, he appears in form in different existences according to the faith and devotion of devotees. He manifests to dispel the darkness of ignorance. When Babaji is referred to as *Mahavatar,* it must be appreciated that it is used as a title of respect and reverence.

There are many *siddhas* who have been associated with him. Prominently mentioned is the historical figure, Hairakhandi Babaji (also written as Haidakhandi, Hairakhan, Hariakhan and other derivatives), about whom there are many references and cited meetings between the 17th century and early 20th century.

An interesting tale is about when Hairakhandi Babaji, along with other *mahatmas,* was visiting Nepal prior to going to Tibet. In those days, the *Raja* of Nepal treated all *sadhus* on a Kailash *yatra* as his personal guests, and would look after their food and clothing requirements during the *yatra*. Accordingly, the *Raja* requested Babaji to look after the *bhandar* or stores for this particular *yatra*, requesting that when stores diminished he should be notified so that they could be replenished. A month passed and Babaji requested no replenishments. Thinking that the *sadhu-sanyasins* would be irked by the lack of hospitality shown to them, the *Raja* visited the camp personally and found the stores still full. With folded hands he requested Babaji to be his permanent '*bhandari*.'

In Kumaon, he is popularly known as Hairakhandi Babaji, from the name of the village Hairakhan or Haidakhan. Locals in the region claim that when he was asked what name they should refer to him as, he had replied, you can refer to me by the name of this village. The Kumaon hills abound with his tales, now mostly hearsay. However, I have met several people who had met him and remember the many miracles that spontaneously occurred in his presence.

Chiranjeevi Kripacharya as well as *chiranjeevi* Ashwasthama, are commonly referred to in relation to him. Even today, in Kumaon, locals who have heard of Hairakhandi Babaji from their fathers, grand-fathers or other elders who had occasion to meet him, say with deep conviction that he is Ashwasthama indeed.

At the beginning of the 20th century, in Nainital, Commissioner Henry Ramsay was going to Court on horseback by Thandi Sarak. Near Pashan Devi, Babaji, who was sitting there, clicked his *chimta* or sacred tongs. The commissioner's horse was distracted and reared suddenly beside the Lake. The commissioner, annoyed at the incident, sent Babaji to the *thana* or local prison, where he was kept behind bars. Going further down the road, the commissioner again saw Babaji ahead. Babaji clicked his *chimta* to the consternation of Commissioner Ramsay. Thoroughly annoyed, he rode to the *thana* to find out why his instructions had not been followed. The subordinate on duty affirmed that Babaji was behind bars and the key was with the *thanapati* in charge, who was immediately summoned. He opened the lock to find a smiling Babaji. Shaken, Ramsay proceeded to the Court where his hand shook as he began to write. He is believed to have said, "I am sorry, I cannot write today," and related the incident in explanation. Later that evening, visiting Babaji, he laid down his cap at his feet.

In another incident, he expressed his disapproval that there were two different paths along the lake, one for Indians and one for British. On a winter day, when British officers and their wives were going on horseback, they saw Babaji beside his *dhuna* on Mall Road itself. This created pandemonium, and the British officers said he should be removed from there forthwith. Babaji scattered *vibhuti* or sacred ash at them and everyone present found themselves stuck to their horses. Completely disconcerted, they were told by Indian officers that they had encountered Babaji and would have to beg his pardon before they would be freed. Accordingly, all of them begged forgiveness and Babaji again scattered *vibhuti* on them, freeing them before he disappeared. This incident was a source of great moral courage and inspiration for the freedom fighters of Kumaon, who realised that Babaji had lent his *shakti* to the cause of Independence.

Another commonly known story is about Jwala Dutt Joshi of Almora, who was at the time Education Minister of Gwalior state. He was riding a horse near Ranibag, where Babaji was at the time working with the labourers. Seeing the '*coolie*' burst into laughter as his horse passed, he was annoyed at his impudence and demanded he be told the cause of the mirth. Babaji explained that he was laughing because in distant Badrinath the bell had fallen and they were having difficulty lifting the heavy bell. Enraged at what he thought was a preposterous bluff, Joshi had a telegram sent to Badrinath and learnt that in truth the incident had occurred. He returned thereafter, to invite Babaji as a state guest of the ruler at the time, Madhavrao Scindia, grandfather of the late Madhavrao Scindia, MP.

While there are legends and tales about Babaji throughout Bharat, connected to different times, the historical figure, Hairakhandi Babaji, who was particularly well known in the Kumaon region of Uttarakhand Himalayas in the late 19th and early 20th century, is possibly the best known and most endearing personality with whom he has been associated. Relatively contemporary, there is a gross physical aspect that people can relate to. Yet when we talk of 'Babaji', it must be remembered that it is not possible to understand the mystery about him, without Divine grace.

CHAPTER 2

Siddha Patal

ॐ

Namaste Adinathaya Vishwanathaye te Namaha
Namaste Vishwarupaya Vishwatithaye Namaha
Utpatti Sthithi Sanghar Karane Klesha Haarane
Namaaste Deva-Deveshwa
Namaste Parmatmane
Yoga Marg Kritetubhyam
Mahayogishwara Pate
Namaste Paripurnayo Jagdananda he Tawe

— *Shloka/Prayer*

Salutations to Adinath, Vishwanath, Vishwarup
Obeisance to the Supreme One
Cause of Creation, Existence, Dissolution
The very end of Suffering
Hail Ye, Supreme God of Gods
Lord Shiva, Yogeshwar of Yogis who reveals Yoga
Thou art All, Thy form is Eternal Bliss

Bhagwan Shiva is the *adi-siddha,* Siddheshwar of all the *siddhas,* or Lord of *Siddhas,* the eternal *siddha.* By his grace does a *yogi* become a *siddha.* Eternal *darshan*, eternal knowledge, eternal bliss, eternal *tejas* or energy are the attributes of a *siddha.* He who is beyond hunger, thirst, heat, cold, sleep, fear, anger, jealousy, attachment, surprise, resentment, anxiety, sorrow, conflict, ego, desire, age, illness, suffering and birth and death is a *siddha,* in truth. Through *tapasya* does a *yogi* ultimately attain to this state of *siddhattwa,* through the grace of Siddheshwar Bhagwan Shankar. Those who are *aviarit purush* or have come to earth by their own will and consciousness are also *siddhas.* They embody purity and freedom.

When this eternal *siddha, niranjan,* beyond all attributes, manifests through divine will in the form of a human being to fulfil the particular needs of a moment in time, the divine descends in human form. To teach the Eternal Truth, Bhagwan Dattatreya, Adi Shankaracharya, Shiva-Gorakshanath, Buddhadev, Rishabdev, Mahavir, Jesus, Moses, Guru Nanak, Mohammad, among others, had manifested.

Achaaro parmo deepo jayate sadhu-sangha maat.

(Divine light in form shines in the presence of *siddhas* or enlightened beings)

The behaviour and character of such a being becomes a source of inspiration for others. The 14 *vidyas* exist within them, in sacred form, not revealed. They are in truth, *Brahma rishis.* Through their own actions, they are exponents of *darshan* or philosophy and exemplify *gyan* or wisdom, *charitra* or character, *tap* or austerity and penance, and *birya* which is *tejas* or divine energy. A *siddha* spontaneously manifests those attributes of perfection and truth that a human being can associate, understand and appreciate as being attributes of revealed perfection. The *siddha* becomes a source of light for humanity to follow. By his action and behaviour he transforms the behaviour of those who emulate him. He is the *acharya* or teacher who defines and determines expected behaviour.

A *sadhu* follows and practices to attain the attributes that manifest spontaneously in a *siddha.* The *sadhu* who seeks liberation and the enlightened state of being undertakes the performance of rigorous discipline, determined practice and severe *tapasya* to achieve that perfection in behaviour, action and character that makes him a worthy contender of spiritual knowledge through the blessings and grace of a *siddha.*

Siddha is immortal, *siddha* swarup is *nirakar-swarup* or formless, beyond attributes, beyond gender. Their field of energy is sacrosanct and esoteric. A *siddha* is one who has no *kaam* or desire, *krodh* or anger, *lobha* or greed, *moha* or attachment and *ahankar* or ego. Such a *siddha* guides *siddha sadhaks* who have total renunciation. *Siddhas* can also work through another, using another body as a medium of work, when they have to enter the field of activity. A *siddha* is one who has *siddha sankalpa,* perfection of resolve, perfection of being, unbound by the world.

It is almost impossible to understand *siddhalok* and *rishilok.* One for whom *samsara* or the world has perished forever, a *siddha,* can attain rishi-hood. While a *rishi* is beyond death, rishis have human manifestation. They are Brahma's *manas putra.* When creation began, the *sapt rishis* were – they are at the beginning of creation and at the end of creation.

They have conquered the *ashtha-dha prakriti* i.e. *panch tattwas* or five elements and three *gunas* or attributes. Maharishi Krishna Dvaipayana Vyasa codified the four *Vedas,* compiled the 18 *Puranas* including the deeply devotional *Srimad Bhagwatam* and wrote the *Mahabharat.* Sri Veda Vyasa is a *maharishi* because he knows all the *lokas* or realms and the divinity and mystery of past, present and future. He has perfect knowledge of *karma, upasana* and *mimamsa,* the path of *karma,* the methods of worship, the wisdom and immortality of the *Vedas.* He is well-versed in practical *yoga, dharma, arth, kaam,* all *shastras* and worldly norms of behaviour.

The legendary Babaji, about whom much has been said, debated, sought and worshipped is a *siddha* of this supreme state. He is the enlightened soul, *param tapaswi, urdhva-retas bramhachari* or one who has conquered all desire, *ashtha-siddhi samparna yogiraj,* or supreme *yogi* with all known *siddhis.*

Babaji, Siddha Babaji, Siddha Gorakhnath, Shiva Baba, Tryambak Baba, Mrityunjay Baba, Sri Manmahamunindra, Sri Satgurudev, Kripacharya, Ashwasthama, Siddha Sunendra-Kunendra, Pahari Baba, Bramhachari Baba, Lama Baba, Sri Mahavatari Baba, Avatari Baba, Mahavatar Baba, Kriya Yoga

Babaji, Hairakhan Haidakhandi Baba, Sri Hari Das, Kanchopi Topa Baba, are some of the many names by which devotees have called this divine being, but not been able to define him or say who he really is.

This legendary master became known as Hairakhandi Baba, Hairakhan Baba, Kanchopi Topa Baba in Kumaon. From the times of the *Mahabharat* till now, what forms has he been known as? Did he exist through all these centuries of time? To understand this, we research and analyse to seek the source wherein the explanations lie. Research and analysis and study while necessary, this truth cannot be understood without overcoming human limitations and undertaking great *tapasya* so that the eternal being with multi-dimensional aspects reveals himself.

At the beginning of the *Ramayana*, the great saint Tulsidas seeks Ma Saraswati and Sri Ganapati's *kripa* or grace before describing Bhawani Shankar as:

Bhawani Shankaro bande shraddha vishwas rupenao

Yabhyam bina na pashyanti siddha swanta-ha stamiswaran

(Salutations to the Supreme Being, Universal Progenitor, Bhawani-Shankar, who is the embodiment of faith and respect, without whose grace even *siddha-lok* itself cannot be enlightened)

We need to be graced with the blessings of Jagdamba Ma Saraswati and Mahaganpati, who bestow knowledge and wisdom. We must have *shraddha* and *vishwas* or respect and faith, the very attributes of Bhawani Shankar who is Uma-Parvati. Through the divine revelation of Mahaprabhu Mahavatar Shiva Matsyendra-Gorakshanath we seek to know his divine form and that *yoga darshan* which is in the realm of deep spiritual insight. The tradition of the Nine *Naths* and 84 *Siddhas* arises from the infinite source of Shiva-Adinath, Shiva-Matsyendra-Gorakshanath.

The *Nath Panth* descrbes the Nine *Naths:*

1. To reveal the *Yoga marg* or path of *Yoga* and to establish

the *siddha* tradition, Lord Shiva Himself manifested in the form of Adinath.

2. Uday Nath is regarded as Mata Parvati. It is Adinath who initiated Uday Nath.
3. *Siddhayogi* Satyanath is regarded as the manifestation of Lord Brahma.
4. *Mahasiddha* Santoshnath among the *Naun Naths* is regarded as an aspect of Lord Vishnu.
5. Achal Achambaynath is regarded as Sheshnag.
6. Gajveli-Gajkantharnath is respected as the form of Lord Ganesh.
7. *Siddha* Chowringhee Nath is regarded as the form of Chandra Devata.
8. Macchendranath, the Matsya *avatar* of Lord Vishnu, is the disciple of Omkar Adinath and believed to be the source of revelation of the *siddha* tradition to mankind.
9. Shiva-Gorakshanath also known as Guru Gorakhnath is the manifestation of Adinath, Lord Shiva. In the *Satya Yuga*, Matsyendranth undertook severe *tapasya* in the jungles of Kamakshya, and here Adinath Lord Shiva gave him *darshan* and offered him a boon. Matsyendranath sought Adinath Himself as his disciple. This promise was fulfilled through Sri Gorakshanath.

Siddhas are ever-existent, beginningless and endless, the very form of Adinath Bhagwan Shankar, the *adi Siddha.* The nine *Naths* include Adinath. The exponent of the form of the tradition of the Nine *Naths* and 84 *Siddhas* has been Shiva-Matsyendra-Gorakshanath. Bhagwan Krishna in the *Gita* had also referred to the nature of *siddhas,* immortal aspects of the divine in form, when he said, "*Siddha naam Kapila Muni*" (Among *siddhas*, I am Kapila Muni). In *Nath Darshan*, Matsyendranath is the form of Narayana-Vishnu and Gorakshanath is the *siddha-avatar* or yogic manifestation of Lord Shiva. When we refer to a *siddha-purush* like Hairakhandi Babaji, who has also been associated with Hairanath, we must seek understanding in relation to the Nine *Naths* and 84 *Siddhas*. The divine *siddha* Hairanath is also believed by devotees to be the manifestation of Gorakshanath.

The eternal sage, Gorakshanath manifests according to the needs of the time. He is not limited to an age or a place, but devotees who have known him in a particular form sometimes find it difficult to transcend that form and realise his eternal timeless nature. His many forms in different times are spoken of with awe, reverence and abiding love among his devotees who are from different cultures and times.

It must also be remembered that there are those divine *siddhas* who history is silent about. Nameless, faceless, they work for the welfare of mankind with a divine *sankalpa* as part of *yogmaya* or divine play, which remains hidden from the curiosity of mortal beings. Only those *yogis* who through intense *tapasya* have attained that realm of being, know and recognise them, and express the divine truths of higher states of consciousness in a form comprehensible to mortal beings, limited by their senses and bound by birth and death. About these divine beings, it is suggested that we seek that Truth through experience born of *tapasya* and grace.

There have been sages and saints worshipped locally within Bharat as well as abroad, who belong to the realm of *siddha-sant patal* and are related to the Himalayas, the eternal playground of higher realms. They are all connected to Bhagwan Shankar. A contextual and contemporary study, without bias and possessiveness, will reveal the nature of divinity associated with this phenomenon. It must be realised that without Lord Shiva and Kailash, his eternal abode, *siddhas* have no identity. Lord Shiva is the powerhouse and source of all energy. Each individual manifestation of consciousness is related to that source, and each is like a bulb, dependent on the energy of the source, without the life energy to manifest without the grace of that divine power.

In talking about Babaji, we are compelled to consider the sentiments of devotees of different temperaments and faith, varied times and cultures, and the many aspects in which saints have taken form in a divine inter-related play where the One becomes Many and the Many in truth is One.

There are some questions that are often asked and that require investigation to be able to understand and know the divine personality associated with all the forms of 'Babaji.' Accordingly one must seek those *yogis* who in their *tapasya* have experienced his grace, or have known his *yoga shakti*, those devotees who have known him as Mrityunjaya Baba, or some of the legends of public appearance or shared experience which require consideration.

The questions raised are:

• Is Shiva-Matsyendra-Gorakshanath's *Mahayoga shakti* manifested through different physical human forms?

• Is this indeed *Bhagwan* Shankar's manifestation?

• Has Guru Kripacharya or Ashwasthama, among the *chiranjeevi* saints, manifested through Hairakhandi Manmunindra Baba either in the past or currently?

• Is Mahavatar Baba, who has never made a public appearance, the manifestation of the collective divinity or *yoga shakti* of Himalayan saints and *siddhas*?

• Could it be possible that Manmunindra Hairakhandi Baba has taken birth in any human form? Or is it possible that he has entered the body of any *yogi* through *shakti diksha* and *kaya-pravesh*?

• What forms have been taken by this divine personality believed by *yogis* to be existent from the *Mahabharat* times?

• Has he maintained a singular identity while remaining immersed in *samadhi*?

• Was he in a state of *samadhi* for over 4000 years until the 17th century from when sightings and experiences have been suggested?

• What have the ancient saints and current saints of the Himalayas to say about this aspect of divinity?

• What is the current thought and acceptance regarding this in *yogic* and philosophical terms?

To answer some of these questions, I undertook an indefinable journey – the journey of life. I visited innumerable sacred places, met many great saints and sages, both known and unknown. In life's journey, we can join the dots in retrospect, but looking ahead, the future remains unknown until we have realised that the future itself is in the past. In this spiritual journey, Maharishi Sri Gorakh Babaji has been my guiding light.

CHAPTER 3

Kripa

ॐ

Guru Brahma Guru Vishnu Gurudeva Maheshwara
Guru Sakshat Para Brahman Tasmay Sri Guruve Namaha
— *Guru Vandana*

The Guru is Brahma, Vishnu, Mahadeva:
creator, sustainer, destroyer
The Guru is ever-existent, eternal. I offer obeisance to the Supreme Guru

The spirit of the Himalayas is reflected through the great *rishis, siddhas* and *yogis* who have done *tapasya* here for nameless ages. Among them, Guru Gorakhnath is mentioned in many scriptures through different traditions. Gorakhnath-ji is widely acknowledged as revealing and maintaining the *siddha* tradition. The presence of *siddhas* is as real as the sun even on a cloud-covered day and the moon even on a moonless night. Among the best known *siddhas* of relatively recent times, Hairakhandi Babaji's presence has often been acknowledged by Himalayan *yogis.*

When I became aware of the continued living presence of *siddhas,* I accepted it as part of the mystery of life that would unravel in the living.

The divine play of life is witnessed spontaneously. It connects us to the very source of joy, of life, of truth, of being, of the unchanging Reality beyond the *maya.* It happens. There is no action, no premeditation. Simply because it is there, it happens and we can be a witness.

The *rishis* and *siddhas* are an undeniable aspect of *yogic* reality. The great *rishis* who have revealed the reality of other dimensions from time to time have been well-grounded in everyday reality. *Rishittwa* is only attained by those spiritually evolved beings who are simultaneously well-versed in the world of mortal man. Maharishi Veda Vyasa sent his son, Sukh Deva-ji, born a realised *yogi*, to *Raja* Janak, for lessons in the world of men and matter. *Videha Raj* Janak, father of Mata Sita, was a realised *yogi* of stature who had the Truth revealed to him through the guidance of Maharishi Ashtavakra as expressed in their dialogues recorded in the *Ashtavakra Gita.* This supreme *Advaita* philosophy is also revealed through the dialogues of Maharishi Vashishtha and his exemplary student, the young Sri Rama, in the *Yoga Vashishtha.*

Through the tapestry or mosaic of life the Truth is revealed. The Infinite cannot be known by the finite, but the body, mind and senses are the medium through which understanding dawns. As awareness grows, we continually discriminate between the temporal and the eternal. We remain absorbed in the Higher Self, while completing actions without attachment. Divinity reveals itself in manifold *maya.*

Through *bhraman* and *sadhana* or spiritual wandering and practice, with the guidance of Sri Gorakh Babaji, I reached Siddhashram in Sitlakhet, where I stayed alone for several days. Sri Gorakh Babaji left with the blessings, "May you have *darshan* of Hairakhandi Babaji." I spontaneously started writing about Hairakhandi Babaji, at whose *tapasya sthals* I have done *sadhana,* whose devotees I have met and known, whose living *samadhi* I have witnessed in the essence of my being, and who has guided me in my own *sadhana* and through many realms of existence. *Siddha patal* is a mystical realm known by *siddhas* and *siddha sadhaks,* occasionally glimpsed by those who are graced to have *darshan* of *siddha-lok.* Otherwise it remains hidden, sacrosanct, mysterious, ever-beckoning.

While there is a physical space and measurable co-ordinates associated with *siddha sthans,* they have nothing to do with physical space, and only *Brahma drishti* or divine vision, which allows one to perceive the subtle, makes it possible to have *darshan* of these divine spaces. The importance of maintaining the sanctity of *shaktipeeths, siddha tapasya sthals* and ancient sacred places of worship cannot be over-stressed. Else, the divinity associated with it is hidden so completely that nothing that happens will affect or awaken those realms, hidden by the *mayic* veil of ignorance. They continue to remain as they are, undisturbed, within dimensions impossible for mortal man to conceive.

And so it is that *Shambala* and *Gyangunj* remain a topic of conversation for the idle curious, a *prateek* or symbol of faith, hope and worship for the devoted and an undeniable reality for those who have been graced to glimpse its eternal formless form.

The 21st century person exposed primarily to physical and material reality, mind disturbed and distracted by the *Kali Yuga*, dismisses the *Puranas* and *Itihaas*, which were once the source of inspiration, as mere stories. The *Smritis* or codes of law are considered arcane. The *Srutis* or *Vedas* are revealed knowledge which remain hidden despite being an open book. *Darshana* or the schools of philosophy are accessible only to the superior intellect of knowledge, understanding and untiring learning. Even then, they remain academic learning unless tempered by practical application. The eternal unchanging truths of the *Upanishads* remain words that can be grasped only at an intellectual level, unless practiced. The spiritual realms remain a dream of an unawakened memory and man struggles to wake to the reality of living.

Where words cannot reach, beyond the vision, beyond the mind indeed, the divine *lila* or play continues, and through it one remains aware of the unchanging reality. To seek those higher truths known in *samadhi*, there are some essential prerequisites. *Shraddha* or respect and faith; *vishwas* or belief and trust; *tapasya* or austerity; *anushthan* or performance of prescribed ritual and form according to the dimension of worship; *satsangha* or the continued exposure to *dharma* or righteous living; and *gyan* or the wisdom born of knowledge.

Through *Karma Yoga* one living in the world can also attain to that state of *yoga.* We can connect to divine energies through *sadhana* and worship, *anushthan, mantra, teerth yatra* and *yoga.*

The great *rishis, siddhas* and *yogis* know and live this Truth. It is not by hearing about them that we can attain to that knowledge, but by following in their footsteps. The *shaktipeeths* and *tapasya sthals* are the corner-stone of transmitting knowledge. *Yatra* and *bhraman* or spiritual journeys increase receptivity. According to one's *yogyata* or readiness to receive and to give, the subtle realms will reveal themselves. This is *anubhuti* or experience and *darshan* or direct knowledge. Whether we merely glimpse the Higher Truth or live continually in the Truth is *kripa* or grace. This is bestowed on the *adhikari* or merit-worthy according to *karma* or actions performed, *sankalpa* or resolved determination and *tapasya* which purifies us.

The truth is ultimately revealed. The composite multi-dimensional consciousness of 'Babaji' has been the *guru* or teacher of many, many *yogis* and *siddhas.* As Bhagwan Dattatreyaya, Shiva Gorakshananth, Adi Shankaracharya-ji have revealed that truth, in more recent times, Hairakhandi Babaji, who has been recognised as *chiranjeevi* Ashwasthama-ji, continues to reveal that truth through *darshan* or direct experience.

The great *yogi* Ashwasthama is the son of Mata Kripi and Maharishi Dronacharya. Kripi is the sister of *chiranjeevi* Kripacharya, *kul guru* of the *Pandavas* and the *Kauravas* of the *Mahabharat.* She is the daughter of Maharishi Sharadwan who is the son of Maharishi Gautam, among the *sapt rishis.*

The *Pandavas* and the *Kauravas* learnt *Dhanur Veda* (*shastra vidya)* or the art and skill of weaponry and warfare from Maharishi Dronacharya. The great warrior, Maharishi Dronacharya is the son of Maharishi Bharadwaj among the *sapt rishis.* Maharishi Bharadwaj is the son of Devguru Brihashpati, *guru* of the *devas.* Devguru Brihashpati is the son of Angiras who comes from Surya Narayan Himself.

The young Ashwasthama was graced by *darshan* of Lord Shiva in childhood. Living in the forests, accustomed to being given rice water as milk, when the boy first tasted cow's milk, rice water was a poor substitute for it. His father offered a tough solution – to do *tapasya* and seek it of Lord Shiva. Tapkeshwar *mandir* in Dehra Dun is the reminder of this ancient legend. In the *Kali Yuga,* water no longer naturally falls on the Shiva *lingam* as it did till recently. Once upon a time, milk had flowed to satisfy the young devotee and it is believed to have continued to flow until a few centuries earlier.

Bhisma Pitamah praises Ashwasthama, son of Drona, as among the foremost *rishis,* creators of that peace and good that men enjoy, in the *Anusasana Parva* of the *Mahabharat.* The great *rishi* and *yogi, maharathi* during the *Mahabharat, chiranjeevi* Ashwasthama is destined to be the Veda Vyasa in the *Dwapar Yuga* of the next 29th *Mahayug,* according to the *Vishnu Purana.* He will also be among the *sapt rishis* in the following 8th *Savarni manvantar* after the current 7th *Vaivaswat manvantar.*

It is *chiranjeevi* Ashwasthama, last acknowledged in the form of Sri Hairakhandi Babaji, who is the inspiration for this book. Sri Gorakh Babaji led me to the many *tapasya sthals* of Hairakhandi Babaji, at each of which he has done *tapasya* himself. He revealed to me the *yogi, siddha* and *rishi parampara* or traditions maintained by the grace of the Divine.

ॐ Namoh Shivaya
ॐ Namoh Bhagwate Vasudevaya
ॐ Sadchidekam Brahma
ॐ Vashishtha adi Sapt Rishibyo Namaha
ॐ Hanuman adi Sapt Chiranjeevibheyo Namaha
ॐ Dattatreyaya Namaha
ॐ Matsyendranathaya Namaha
ॐ Gorakshnathaya Namaha
ॐ Naun Nath Churasi Siddhon Namaha
ॐ Ashwasthamaya Namaha
ॐ Manmunindra Sri Hairakhaneshwaracharyaya Namaha
ॐ Gurubhyo Namaha, ॐ Gurubhyo Namaha

sadhana

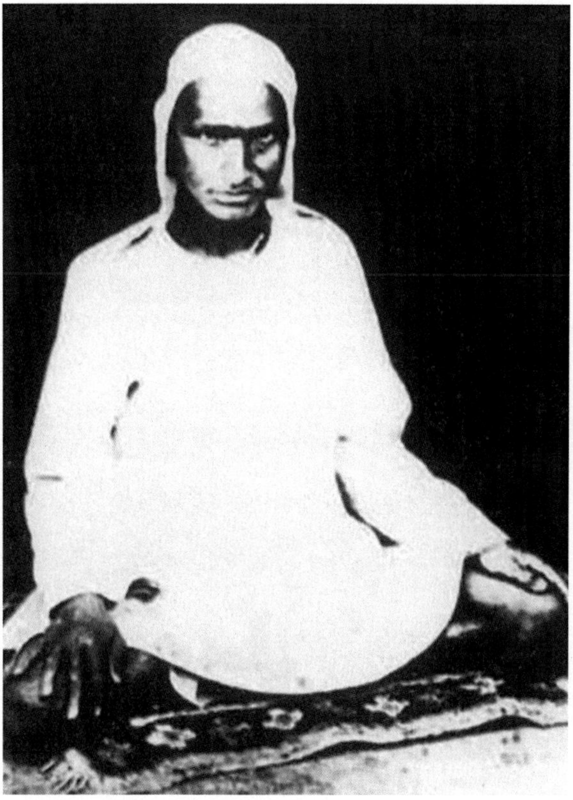

Hairakhan Babaji
affectionately called Kanchopi Toṗa Ḃaba in Uttarakhand

Sri Sombari Babaji

CHAPTER 4

Maneshwar

ॐ

Vande Deva Uma-Patim Surgurum
Vande Jagadkaranam
Vande Pannag Bhushanam Mrigdharam
Vande Pashunapatim
Vande Surya Sashank Bahir Nayanam
Vande Mukundapriyam
Vande Bhaktjana Sayang cha Vardham
Vande Shivam Shankaram

— *Shiva Vandana*

Pranam to Uma-Patim, Lord of Lords
Hail to the Cause, Effect and Dissolution
Salutations to the one who wears a garland of snakes and deerskin
Hail to the Lord of All Creation
Praise be to the One whose eyes are the Sun and the Moon
Hail to Mukundapriyam, Beloved of Lord Krishna
Obeisance to the One who shelters his devotees and grants boons
I bow in reverence to Lord Shiva-Shankar

Arriving at the familiar Kathgodam station, yet another journey through time began. Sri Gorakh Babaji led me along many trails of Hairakhandi Babaji. We visited different *tapasya sthals* and sacred places of worship, frequented in the past by Hairakhandi Babaji, where Sri Gorakh Babaji has also done *sadhana* or spiritual practice, *tapasya* or austerities and *anushthan* or worship according to the ancient traditions.

We drove into the Himalayas, stopping briefly at Sri Sombari Babaji's *ashram* at Padampuri and at one of Sri Gorakh

Babaji's current *tapasya sthals* at Paharpani, both of which were also frequented by Hairakhandi Babaji in the late 19th and early 20th centuries. Thereafter, we paid our respects at the Devi Dhura *mandir.* Hairakhandi Babaji would stay at Machwal or *rishi* Muchkunda's *ashram* where many *rishis* have done *tapasya,* and where Devi's *doli* or palanquin returns to her *maika* or ancestral home the day after *Raksha Bandhan,* the one day in the year she is taken out of her copper resting place. On *Raksha Bandhan,* the *buggal* or stone-fight is scheduled during the week-long *mela* or Festival here to coincide with the *darshan* of Devi.

4 miles from Devi Dhura, visible on the peak ahead, is Garg Chula, where *siddha* Airi Deva, among the *Panchnama Devas,* regarded as the incarnation of Arjun of the *Mahabharat,* had done *tapasya.* Ahead of Devi Dhura is Phatak Shila, another *siddhapeeth* of Airi Deva, where *rishi-munis* have done *tapasya.* It is customary for *siddhas* and *siddha sadhaks* to spend time in *sadhana* and *tapasya* at these sacred places. There is possibly no *siddha sthan* in Kumaon where Hairakhandi Babaji had not spent time. He had visited here on many occasions when it was not connected by road. Sri Gorakh Babaji, who has done *tapasya* here and at innumerable *siddha sthans,* confirms that even today, spending time in *tapasya* can elevate one's state of consciousness creating deep spiritual insight by which one can experience the subtle realms of the *siddhas* and have their *darshan.* I am personally aware of these elevated states of consciousness that happen spontaneously as grace in the presence of *siddhas.*

We stayed the night at Khetikhan, one of the many places at which Hairakhandi Babaji had also stayed in the past, mostly at Narsingh Danda or Siddha Chula, borne out by tales of old-timers. Swami Vivekananda too had spent a night here and considered building an *ashram* before proceeding to Mayavati, 4 miles ahead, where the *Advaita ashram* was built.

Early in the morning, we visited the *ashram* at Maneshwar

between Lohaghat and Champavat. Here, hundred year old Mahant Daya Krishna Puri-ji of the Sola Madhi Bhagwan Puri Dariyab, Mahanirmani Akhada, known as Thanapati-ji, lived. From the road, walking a km along a paved pathway through the forest, we came to the *ashram.*

The *lingam* at Maneshwar is *swayambhu* or self-existent, not established by anyone. It is believed that the *tapasya* of some ancient *rishi* would have caused the manifestation of the *lingam* as a blessing of Lord Shiva. The *mandir* was built by the Chand *rajas* of Champavat.

There is a *naula* or underground source of water which leads to a *kund* beside the temple. This *kund* is much like Badrinath, except that the water is cold. Sri Gorakh Babaji took water from the *kund* for a bath, before going into the temple to offer worship. I did likewise.

Behind the temple are the *samadhis* of the different *sanyasins* who have lived here, including the living *samadhi* of Siddha Baba Bhairav Giri-ji, the first in a long line to head this *ashram.* A live *samadhi* is when an accomplished *yogi,* an adept, voluntarily gives up the body to merge in Consciousness. Among *yogis,* this is a known practice, and there are several instances of living *samadhis.*

It is rare when a *siddha yogi* takes living *samadhi* and dissolves the body. There have been historical instances where the body was not found. It is said that in place of Kabir's body, there were flowers. A *siddha* who merges with universal consciousness can take a body, as and when required through the manifestation of divine will. A well known instance is the legend of Sri Matsyendranath who gave *vibhuti* in blessing to a barren woman. Fearing ridicule, she discarded it in the *gobar* or dung heap. Twelve years later, when Matsyendranath came looking for his disciple, the young Gorakshanath appeared where the *vibhuti* had been scattered. It is stated that Sri Matsyendranath sought his disciple as a boon when he received *darshan* of Lord Shiva.

To take *jal samadhi or him samadhi,* to merge the elements

of the body into water or in the Himalayan snows is the way of rare Himalayan *yogis.* It is believed that Hairakhandi Babaji, in the tradition of *rishis* and *siddhas,* did that. It must be kept in mind that he is regarded as the *chiranjeevi* Ashwasthama, who will be the Veda Vyasa of the next *mahayug* at the time of the following *Dwapar Yuga.* He will be responsible for recording spiritual history and revealing the Truth of the *Srutis,* just as Krishna Dwaipayana Vyasa, has done in compiling the *Vedas* and the *Puranas,* and recording the history of an age through the *Mahabaharat.* The *Vishnu Purana* declares this and records Ashwasthama's name among the *sapt rishis* of the next *manvantar.* We are not talking simply about a saint here, we are referring to a *siddha yogi* of supreme stature, an eternal *rishi. Siddhas* are those supreme *yogis* about whom almost nothing is ever known. The *rishis* have taken form throughout recorded *Puranic* history. In their presence, the limitations of possible and impossible disappear.

When we talk of the *Mahabharat* with ordinary mortal understanding, we undermine the fact that it is about a time when Lord Krishna, who is Lord Vishnu, on whom the world rests, descended to Earth. With Him, all who came to participate in the divine *lila,* were *yogis* and *rishis* of stature.

When the *Pandavas* went to Veda Vyasa asking him to suggest what must be done to atone for that earned by living and engaging in the epic battle, the great Maharishi Veda Vyasa indicated that only *darshan* of Lord Shiva could absolve them. And so they sought Bhagwan Shankar's *darshan* as He eluded them through the Panch Kedar. Eventually, the *Pandavas* with Draupadi went into the Himalayas towards Kailash in *tapasya.* It must be kept in mind that Yudhishthir was the son of *Dharma Raj* – the embodiment of righteousness and Truth. Arjun was a *yogi* of superior stature, guided by Lord Krishna Himself, the Supreme One. Bhima, like *chiranjeevi* Sri Hanuman, was *Pavan-putra* – son of the Wind. Each of the five *Pandavas* were sought from the gods through a boon and therefore represent the manifestation of a divine energy.

Draupadi, beloved of the *Pandavas*, is among the *Panch Kanyas*, worshipped by tradition, who lives in the hearts of the people of Bharat, remembered through the re-telling of the *Mahabharat*.

Yogis, *rishis* and *siddhas* who remain merged in consciousness, donned bodies. *Avatarit purusha* who descend to earth of their free will were the divine witnesses. The great *maharathi* Bhisma Pitamah, one of the eight *Vasus*, paid his *karmic* debt in taking form, finally leaving his body at will. His mother is the very Ganga herself, who took form because it was decreed that she must be born. After the birth of Bhishma, she merged into the river again, but is yet believed to have brought up the young Bhishma whose *guru* was *chiranjeevi* Sri Parasuram, among the *Dasavatar* of Lord Vishnu.

Ganga, as the sacred river, sought through *tapasya* by *Maharaja* Bhagirath, remains in *samadhi* as pure energy, while absolving man, and even the gods themselves, of their mortal form. Ganga remains in *samadhi* as the sacred waters in Lord Brahma's *kamandal*. This divine energy would have destroyed the Earth if Lord Shiva Himself had not released her through his matted locks. Who is this great Ganga, in *yogic* terms, daughter of Brahma, constant companion of Lord Shiva, but Devi Herself. Just as Gayatri is the embodiment of the goddess of wisdom, the mighty Saraswati, consort of the Creator Brahma. Among the great warriors of the *Mahabharat* were *kulguru chiranjeevi* Sri Kripacharya, and his sister's son, *chiranjeevi* Sri Ashwasthama, son of Drona, both of whom are destined to witness the passing *yugas*. *Chiranjeevi* Krishna Dwaipayana Vyasa is the witness who has recorded the divine *lila* to reveal this Supreme Truth to mankind in this age.

When we talk of *mahatmas* like Hairakhandi Babaji, we must remember them in connection with the various associations, so we can transcend our limited mortal ego in seeking their *darshan* to understand the divinity of their manifest energy.

Hairakhandi Babaji was a visitor at Maneshwar during Siddha Babaji's time, and probably both before and after that. Since the time of Siddha Baba Bhairav Giri, the *pujaris* or priests of the temple at Maneshwar have been *sanyasins.* Thanapati-ji lived in Siddha Baba's *kutia* which is maintained in the ancient tradition, cleansed daily with *gobar* and *mitti* – cowdung and earth. It is the traditional *mahatma's kutia,* austere, with the main features being the ancient *dhuna* and an area of worship. Nearby are a few other dwelling places for visiting saints and others.

Thanapati-ji had received *darshan* of Hairakhandi Babaji in his childhood in his village near Gangolihat. I wanted to know more about Hairakhandi Babaji. A mere handful of people today can talk about their personal experiences of meeting the historical personality known as Hairakhandi Babaji.

It was a delight to talk to Thanapati-ji. The difference between talking about Hairakhandi Babaji to a *sanyasin* and to others is simply that the *sanyasin* focuses on the wisdom he gained from the meeting, whereas others talk of miracles. I have seen how an event I have witnessed is viewed entirely differently by various people. It is true that in the presence of *siddhas,* 'miracles' occur, but so spontaneously, and so naturally, that it can only be appreciated as divine will and not an individual's action. There is a vast difference between *siddhis* that have been acquired on the spiritual path either spontaneously or through particular *sadhana,* and the *siddhis* of *siddhas.* It is important to differentiate between them. There is also a difference between *vibhuti* or miracles on the spiritual path and spontaneous occurrences around *siddhas. Siddhas* are so completely beyond the usual gross worldly planes of living, that their actions and words can only be understood with purity of vision.

Hairakhandi Babaji's simplicity is legendary. Once when he was visiting a poor devotee, he asked him what happened to the home he had intended to build for himself. The devotee said that being alone, and not having money to pay for the labour, he had been unable to build it. Babaji stayed on to carry slabs of stones and help his devotee build his home.

Thanapati-ji was happy to talk about Hairakhandi Babaji. He said, two things stood out about him, one was his attitude of '*mein hi mein*', absorbed in the Self, and the other was '*mein aur tu mein bhed nahin*', no difference between you and me. When he spoke he did not try to create a sense of satisfaction in the other, but only spoke to express the *gyan* or wisdom of his being. Thanapati-ji said, "Today, *sadhus* speak words that are pleasing to hear, they cater to the audience they address, true saints only speak the Truth."

About Hairakhandi Babaji, he said, "he never saw any negative in anyone, he never saw the faults and blemishes. I learnt that God does not look at our *paap* and *aparadh* or sins of omission and commission. We should not think, I have sinned and remain in that negative. We should focus on how we can repair the damage done, how we can change our behaviour. We should atone for it through positive action, through remembering the name of God. When we remember our sins, which we will from time to time, we should replace the thought with that which will atone for the sin. *Punya ke samne paap nahin rehta*, in the face of virtue, vice no longer remains."

Thanapati-ji said, "A human weakness that most of us suffer from, is our need for appreciation, for status, for respect by the other. Hairakhandi Babaji never had this trait. He respected the other so completely that there were occasions he took the blame for something that was done by another so that the other would not lose face. He believed that in respecting another, Narayana himself was being respected." With this, Thanapati-ji's voice broke and his eyes filled with tears. He said "I cannot speak of him or think of him without feeling great emotion. What a blessing it was to meet him as a child. If only I had known and understood the greatness of his being then, where would I be today."

When taking his leave, seeking Sri Gorakh Babaji's permission, I promised Thanapati-ji I would return. Sri Gorakh Babaji assured Thanapati-ji that he himself would be returning. Weeks after I met him, I learnt that Thanapati-ji had left his mortal body. Return I must, if it be so destined. When I am there again, perhaps I will know what remains – whether I met Thanapati-ji in conclusion of a pre-appointed destiny, or whether I have already promised him another meeting that must be fulfilled.

Chapter 5

Devi Dhura & Paharpani

ॐ

Na Mantram no Yantram tadapi cha na janey Stuti Maho
Na chavanam Dhyanam tadapi cha na janey Stuti Katha
Na jane Mudraaste tadapi cha na janey Vilapanam
Param janey Matastwadanusarnam klesha haranam
– Devi Apradh Kshama Stotram by Shankaracharya

Oh mother, ignorant of mantras and yantras
Without the words and form of prayers
Unable to invoke you or to meditate on you
Without the right words of praise
I know not mudras
Nor methods of worship and farewell
Yet I remember you as a child calls his mother
I know you, who dispels all sorrow and conflict

At the conclusion of the week long Devi Dhura *mela*, on *Raksha Bandhan*, when sister's tie a sacred thread on the wrist of brothers with a prayer of protection for them, the *buggal* or heroic stone-fight is held in time-honoured tradition. Some fifty villages participate, having kept a fast and taken the blessings of Devi. The heroes among them take part in this battle where participants gather in the four *khams* of Garhwal Kham, Chimwal Kham, Walik Kham, Lamgarhia Kham and seven *tokes* or regions. Congregating according to their villages, representing the four directions, they assemble in battle formation from two sides. Armed with giant protective shields, they fling stones at each other in symbolism of *Dharma Yudh* or righteous war, fought without subterfuge. It is customary to continue the fight until an equivalent of one man's blood has been shed by the injured, after which the warriors gather together in friendship again. For the 40 minutes or more of the battle, witnessed by thousands from neighbouring villages, a hush descends on the crowd as the battle is fought in right earnest.

Devi Dhura has an ancient Gabori and Bhagwati Barahee *mandir*, and is among the 108 *shakti peeths*, where Sri Durga Mata is believed to be ever-present. In honour of her devotees, on this one day in the year, accompanied by great fanfare and ceremony, the *murti* of Devi comes out from her resting place where she resides through the year.

According to folklore, Devi Dhura was visited by the *Pandavas* of the *Mahabharat*. Bhim, who did *tapasya* here, received *darshan* of Devi. There is a huge rock, Bhim *shila*, symbolic of this incident.

On the way back from Devi Dhura, I stopped at Paharpani where I spent a few days in solitude and *sadhana*, or spiritual practice. Paharpani is within the mighty Himalayas, at the border of Nainital and Almora districts. On the ancient pilgrim trail, it is picturesque and pristine. Geographically, it is in the evergreen forests, with *banj (oak), brus* (rhododendron), *chir* (pine), *devadar* and *kaphal*. At a height of 6,500 -7,000 feet, this is a valley of fruits: pear, plum, peach, apricot, walnut, lime, orange.

The mighty Himalayan peaks can be viewed at various places, one to three 3 kms away. They are also visible in all their grandeur from nearby places, like Managher,10 km behind. On the road towards the Himalayan peaks of Nanda Khat, Nandakot, Nanda Ghunti, Nandachuli, Trishul, these peaks can be seen from Motia Pathar 3 km; Punagarh 6 km; Gajaar 7 km; Durganagar 8 km; Sahar Phatak 10 km; Mournaulla 13 km; Airi Deva 18 km; Siddha Beri Chula 26 km and Devi Dhura 40 kms from Paharpani.

Paharpani is connected to several places of pilgrimage and beauty in the districts of Nainital, Almora and Pithoragarh. Via Almora, onto Karanprayag, it is possible to go onto the *Char Dham* of Garhwal: Badrinath, Kedarnath, Gangotri and Yumnotri.

At Paharpani, at a distance of 1 km below the road, is an ancient *mahagufa.* It is also known as *gupt gufa,* or among the sacred secret caves of the Himalayas. In this *mahagufa* or complex of caves, there are several caves which can be used for purposes of intense *sadhana.* The chief *gufa* is deep and the path is narrow and perilous, making it virtually impossible to go far within.

Close to the *gufa* is Sri Gorakh Babaji's *tapasya dhuni,* called Manasarovar Kailash *dhuni* where five *siddhas,* the Panchnama Devas or *siddha* Gorakhnath with Dattatreya, Airi Deva, Gorril Deva, Shyamjyu Deva and Harjyu Deva, have been invoked in sacred *siddha* worship. At a *dhuni,* all the *deva-devis* are worshipped in their *nirakar swarup* or eternal form. *Siddha dhunis* are graced by Lord Shiva, and his sacred symbols of protection like the *trishul* or trident, *chimta* or sacred tongs, *khadga* or sword, *dhanush-baan* or bow and arrow, and *paori* or axe, stand witness to this. At this *dhuni,* Hairakhandi Babaji's ancient *chimta,* presented by a villager of Kooni to Sri Gorakh Babaji is part of the *shakti* or divine power present here. Another *chimta* here, is from the Gorakhnath *dhuni* at Graoun, Saalam. This was presented to Sri Gorakh Babaji by the old *pujari,* Pandit Nityananda Joshi, who had a vision during his *tapasya kaal,* in which Sri Gorakhnath appeared to him directing him to do so.

The rules governing a *siddha dhuna* are very strict and the ancient traditions are maintained. People should not attempt to go near a *siddha dhuna.* A *tapaswi yogi* does not enter his own *dhuna* without first awakening the energies within himself.

Within the *gufa,* where the villagers come to worship, a

small *murti* of Devi, and symbols of Ganesh-ji, Bhairav Nath, and a Shiva *lingam* from Alaknanda, Badrinath have been consecrated by Sri Gorakh Babaji. At the small *dhuna* in the *gufa* temple is an ancient *diya*, presented to Sri Gorakh Babaji by the late Liladhar Bughani.

Next to this *gufa*, is a cave known as *bagh gufa* or *naga gufa*. It has been so named because during Sri Gorakh Babaji's prolonged *tapasya* here, a *bagh* or leopard stayed here, as also a Naga Deva, or sacred snake, protectors of *tapaswi yogis* during their *tapasya kaal*. Nearby is Sri Gorakh Babaji's small *kutia* or dwelling place, *Dasnama Sanyas Kutir*, where he lives during his *tapasya kaal* here. Close to the *kutia*, there is a large *yogini gufa*, where a *bagh* or leopardess comes to nurture her cubs. When Babaji's *kutia* did not have doors, in his absence, the leopardess and cubs would take shelter here. Ahead of the *kutia* is the *yagya sthan* where Sri Gorakh Babaji has held *yagya* for the nearby villagers and performed *anusthan*. Many local people became thus aware of this sacred cave.

In this *mahagufa*, Mahavatar Hairakhandi Babaji, among other *yogis*, have done *tapasya* at a time when this was in the deep dense forests, before there was any village settlement nearby. Legend claims this was also used by the *Pandavas* in the days of the *Mahabharat*.

Hairakhandi Babaji would go on foot from this *gufa* via Kooni village to the river, Ghatkar, three kms below. The Ghatkar later joins the Gautumi Ganga river in the Kumaon Kailash region. Sri Hairakhandi Babaji would go through Nain Gaon to his cave at Devguru Brihaspati. There is now a road from Paharpani to Mournaulla and onto Bherapani from where there is a 7 km trail to Devguru Brihaspati, a sacred *tapasya sthal*, where Brihaspati, the *guru* of the *devas* or the gods, is believed to have done prolonged *tapasya*. From here, Babaji would take the trail to Tushrar village, and via Takura, would visit the Siddheshwar *mandir* which is also known as Gautum Rishi's *ashram*. He would then proceed onto his cave at Hairakhan, from where he became known as Hairakhandi

Babaji by the nearby villagers.

As is spoken of Patal Bhuvaneshwar beyond Haat Kalika, which has now been made public, there are supposed to be pathways leading to several places of pilgrimage like Kashi and Haridwar. So also it is said that there are *yogic marg* or pathways from the Paharpani *gufa* which lead to Haridwar and Kumaon Kailash. It must be realised that these *margs* are for *yogis* and *siddhas*, and not for the general public, and so come into the mystical realms of *siddhashram.*

The late Liladhar Bughani, son of Nardeva Bughani of Bughani Estate, Paharpani personally knew both Hairakhandi Babaji and Sombari Babaji. He was a regular visitor at the *gufa* where he would perform *Devi paath* during *Navaratri* when Sri Gorakh Babaji was there. Once as he sat on a stone alone near Babaji's *dhuni,* he heard rumbles from within the *gufa* and ran away in fright. Villagers come to offer worship at most *tapasya sthals.* They do not tarry however, and rarely is anyone willing to be alone. In many instances, *sadhu-sanyasins* who are doing *sadhana* and *tapasya* have been compelled to leave without completing their *sadhana,* and fearful tales abound. It is firmly believed that a *siddha tapasya sthal* will not allow anyone but a *siddha* or *a siddha sadhak* to remain. Certainly, I have heard numerous hair-raising stories of terror, some told by very serious practitioners, who are neither gullible nor overly susceptible to machinations of the mind. Bughani-ji had many stories to tell, heard from his father and his grandfather, both about Hairakhandi Babaji, and about Sombari Babaji who used to live mainly at Padampuri and Kakrighat.

Near Bughani Estate is the *samadhi* of Swami Trilochananda Giri-ji, who had made a Shiva *mandir* near his *kutia* and *dhuni.* Trilochananda-ji would also speak of Hairakhandi Babaji, whose *darshan* he received as a child at Puhao Dewal at Saalam, where both Hairakhandi Babaji and Sombari Babaji had attended a *yagya.* Later, inspired by this *darshan,* he took *sanyas.*

At Paharpani, a veteran freedom fighter, Pandit Lokmani

Sharma, close to a century now, recalls his early childhood when Hairakhandi Babaji would visit his ancestral home at Kooni village. He tells stories of how Babaji would ask them to prepare *mudgua ka roti* made of a local black wheat flour, and *shishumna ka sag*, an unusual delicacy made from a thorny stinging nettle which grows in the area. Sri Babaji would say he was going to bathe at Haridwar. He would disappear from some 20-30 yards away to reappear there in time for his meal.

Another story told about him is that while playing with the children he would sit with a wet cloth draped on him within a heap of dry grass and alighting it, would take *agni samadhi*, disappearing from vision. According to Sharma-ji, he would later emerge looking like a red-hot golden orb and then reappear in his physical form before the children. It must be kept in mind that unable to explain their mystical experience, people commonly speak of the experience in terms of light and a miraculous phenomenon. For mortal man, the divine light is almost impossible to behold without becoming temporarily blinded.

Till 1920-22, Sri Hairakhandi Babaji was regularly seen by villagers as he moved in natural physical form. It is generally cited that his last public appearance was when he travelled from his Kathgaria *ashram* to Hairakhan *dham*, Kumaon Kailash before proceeding to Askot, where he stayed as the guest of the *raja* of Askot of the Katyuri dynasty. In an earlier incident, it is said that the *raja*, a keen devotee, had sent word to Hairakhandi Babaji requesting *darshan* for an important British officer in His Majesty's service. When Babaji had refused it, the *raja* had sent the officer to Hairakhandi Babaji who was at the time either at Hamseshwar Mahadeva or Mallika Arjuna, both Shiva *shaktipeeths*, nearby. Babaji became *antardhyana*, disappearing from there. That night, the Raja was shaken off his bed, believed to be because of Babaji's displeasure.

After his final visit at Askot, Babaji's ceremonial departure was in a *palki* or palanquin. As already intimated by him, he disembarked from the *palki* at Jauljebi on the banks of the *sangam* of the rivers Kali and Gauri. Here, eye witnesses reported that he was last seen mid-stream with his head emerging amidst the rapid waters, after which he was not seen again. It is said that he had already indicated that he would be taking eternal *samadhi* by disintegrating his elemental body. It is believed that he took *samadhi* either here or at Manasarovar-Kailash. Till about 1940, individual devotees or a small group of devotees have claimed to have seen him occasionally, for brief spells, in the same physical form. It is believed that this was through his *yogic* power to appear and disappear at will.

Chapter 6

Along the Trail

ॐ

Paani behta bhala, Yogi chalta bhala

– Sadhu Bani (old saying of sanyasins)

As water must flow to retain its purity, a yogi must roam

Early one morning, sitting at the Gabori *gufa* at Paharpani, absorbed in the *Nada* or cosmic vibration, I completed my spiritual practices. I grew aware of a rhythmic step in the distance, and of the *prana* of an approaching *yogi*. I stepped out of the *gufa* to meet Sri Gorakh Babaji who had just reached Paharpani. He was on his way to Sombari Babaji's *ashram* at Padampuri, where he had left a message that we would be reaching in a few hours. Accordingly, I returned to Pandit Lokmani Sharma's dwelling where I was staying, and bid farewell to the centurion and his family.

Our first halt that day was scheduled for Padampuri. We made innumerable stops and Babaji spoke to the several villagers we met en route. Children were asked the names of their fathers and grandfathers and told to inform them at home that Babaji would be coming that way again. With the men, he talked about the seasonal crops and exchanged local news. He exchanged greetings with the women we met, and asked which village each was from. Sometimes he stopped briefly at a home where someone had passed away recently or stopped to meet someone old or ailing.

Near Dhanachuli, Babaji asked at a shop on the road about a particular gentleman. We were told he had gone out in his car. Babaji said, "okay, take me to his house, so I can talk to you the while." With that, we met the gentleman's sister-in-law, who welcomed us into her neighbouring home saying that we had come on a good day, being her late sister's birthday. She had been grieving the loss of her dearly beloved sister, when they lost her nephew, the gentleman's 28 year old son, in an air crash. She spoke of her brother-in-law's stoicism.

She greeted us with the warmth and welcome reserved for a passing *sanyasin,* though she was not aware of it herself, living in a cultural and social background removed from this ancient tradition. Instead she greeted us as though we were guests she had hoped would be arriving. On our way out, we learnt that the gentleman whom Babaji had stopped to meet, had returned.

His hair was silver grey and his eyes reflected the human suffering he had known. He asked me, "why do you look so familiar, tell me where we have met, I feel somehow I am meeting my sister." I stayed silent, though I could perhaps have explained it to him. It was still close to *Raksha Bandhan.* Being currently without preoccupation of the personal self, I was reflecting the sentiments and the energy of the festival itself. I had been to Devi Dhura, possibly the most energised space for *Raksha Bandhan,* and thereafter, spent three nights in *sadhana* at Paharpani. Yes, I could have explained why he was so sure he was meeting his sister. I was the impersonal sister. Soon, like the passing wind, we had left their homes.

I was keen to climb uphill to Jilling, which I had been told was a possible community dwelling place for several people who had enlisted me to do the needful and check it out. Babaji took 3 steps on the path up and said, *"Yeh tumlog ke bas ke nahin hai."* I knew he was referring to city dwellers with fantasies of Himalayan living. I quietly said that I would like to see the place anyway. We walked on.

I had forgotten that I was walking now in remote

Himalayan villages where a passing *sadhu* is rarely ignored. Beside one hut, a woman called to say, "Babaji, you look like a real saint, as though you have *gyan,* do you have knowledge of herbs and medicines?" Babaji was in a jocular mood. He replied, "I have *lavang, elaichi, supari,* if you take out your old *tamba* (copper vessels), I will exchange them for new, that's the kind of *sadhu* I am." He was allowed to proceed on.

We had walked up a continuous incline for more than half an hour when we came to another hut. Here, the old lady would not let Babaji go. "Can you see the future, can you find the lost?" she queried, barring his path.

He replied, "I can't do anything."

The old lady was disbelieving, "You look like a great saint, will you solve my problems?"

We had not even had a chance to take a breath from the climb up. He said, "When you meet a shopkeeper on the road, do you ask him for provisions? Visit my *dhuni* instead." She immediately wanted to know where he had come from. Babaji said, "Padampuri."

She asked, "will you be there if I come there?"

"Yes, certainly," he replied, adding that if he is not there, someone else will be there.

She was determined that only he could answer her question. "You must have tea," she said, explaining that we had only reached half way up. There and then I abandoned the mission of going ahead. We refused tea and opted for apples from the trees instead. The old lady asked if her son who had been gone some 15 years would ever return. "Can you make him return," she pleaded.

He admonished her for crying over a son lost so long, instead of enjoying her two other sons and her grand-children. She was inconsolable. Looking into the distance, he said, "He is well. He has married and had a family."

"But will he return?"

"Yes, he will come here again," was the reply.

"When?"

"That I cannot tell you. But he will come. And now be happy with these grand-children who surround you, with all that you have."

Her daughter-in-law ran in to get *dakshina.* Babaji said, "Why should I take *dakshina* from the poor?" He reached in his pocket and taking out a note, handed it to the youngest child in his grand-mother's lap. The daughter-in-law pleaded that she was on her Monday fast, and had just returned from the temple. "Give me that cucumber growing on the plant, instead," he said. She quickly climbed down to get him the largest cucumber, but insisted on giving him *dakshina* as well. Finally he relented, and smiled as he showed them his pocket saying, "my pockets are so large, I can take any amount of *dakshina.*"

At the entrance Babaji turned to say, "Your son must have been your enemy in a previous life, else why would he leave you with no word and cause you so much grief. Forget him immediately and enjoy those who love you." Nothing Babaji had said earlier had relieved her of her anxiety as did these words. She nodded and was ready to let him leave.

We walked back quickly to where the trail met the main road. As the afternoon faded we drove through Bhowali, as dusk gathered we passed Ranikhet, as the darkness of night settled we drove to Siddhashram, Sitlakhet. Paying our respects at the *mandir* there, Babaji stayed overnight, leaving at dawn, saying, "A river must flow and a *yogi* must roam."

Chapter 7

Sombari Babaji's Ashram, Padampuri

ॐ

Dhrishti sthir yasya vina Sadrishyam
Vayu Sthiro yasya Vina Prayatnam
Chitta sthir yasya Vinavalambam
Sa Brahmataraantaranaadarupa
—Nadabindu Upanishad - verse 56

When vision becomes fixed without any object to be seen
When Vayu (Prana) becomes still without effort
When the Chitta becomes firm without support
He becomes of the form of the subtle sound of Brahma-Pranava.

Before we went towards Jilling, we had stopped at Sombari Babaji's *ashram*, Padampuri. 116 year old Swami Parmananda Puri was sitting outside in the sun, on his asana on a *chatai*. The last two times I had visited here, each time the conversation turned to particular topics which I wanted to talk to him about, there was a disturbance and we could not continue.

A few days earlier, we had stopped here on the way to Maneshwar where Thanapati-ji Maharaj lived. Swami Parmananda-ji had spoken of his *darshan* of Sri Hairakhandi Babaji in 1938-'39 at the home of Guman Singh Naula of Kurmapur, Deola, known as Gumani Bhagat. While Hairakhandi Babaji was last seen publicly around 1920, there are accounts of his having met devotees briefly till about 1940. It is generally believed among *yogis* that these brief appearances

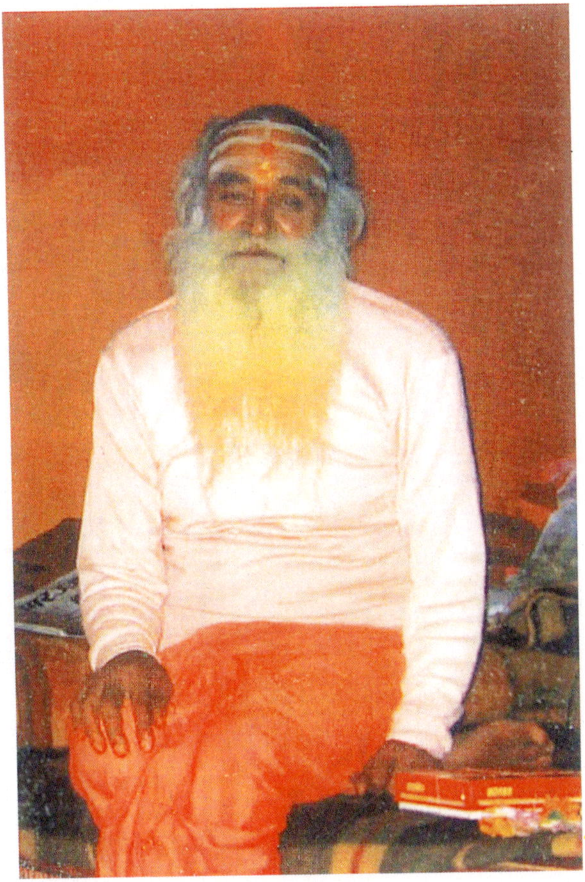

Thanapati Puri-ji at Maneshwar

Swami Parmananda Puri-ji
at Sombari Babaji's ashram, Padampuri

Swami Parmananda Puri-ji with Sri Gorakh Babaji

in the physical body by which he was known, were through his *yogic* power to materialise and dematerialise the body. It is widely believed that he took living *samadhi* after he was last publicly sighted after a visit to Askot.

Swami Parmananda-ji spoke of his evening's meeting more than 65 years ago, when Sri Hairakhandi Babaji, Gumani Bhagat and he were present. He said that he asked Babaji a single question, "*what is the pehchan of a tattwa-gyani or atman-gyani?*" (How can one recognise one who has overcome the elements, and knows the Self?)

Sri Hairakhandi Babaji had replied, there is no *'tol'* of such a one, no balance by which he can be measured. However there are some *'lakshans'* or indications. An *atman gyani* sees no '*dosh*' or fault in anyone, and he speaks no ill of anyone.

The next day when I visited Thanapati-ji at Maneshwar he echoed the very same sentiments in uncanny repetition when speaking of Sri Hairakhandi Babaji. whose *darshan* he had received several times as a child in his ancestral village near Gangolihat.

Now, wasting no time, I told Sri Paramananda-ji that I was writing a book about Himalayan saints, and wanted to talk to him. His mind totally focused, he said, "What will I speak of the gross? I will talk the language of the spirit." I was ready to receive what he said. "I have come thrice to receive this", I replied.

Sri Gorakh Babaji, who had stopped at the shops nearby, now arrived with fruits for Swami Parmananda-ji, and they greeted each other with warmth. Then I witnessed a play now so familiar – the play of *siddhas.* The highest Truths are spoken in the simplest way – this is the *sahaj samadhi* Sri Hairakhandi Babaji was a *marg darshak* of, one who shows the path towards.

In the midst of this palpable energy, Sri Gorakh Babaji, instead of maintaining the austere silence that the situation demanded, became extremely playful and child-like. While Sri Parmananda-ji, obviously in deep contemplation, tried to convey the inexplicable, Sri Gorakh Babaji said, "why should I lie?" Parmananda-ji looked at him as though something of grave importance would be revealed. Babaji again repeated, *"Jhoot kyon boloon?"* His next sentence would have made me laugh aloud, but I was too absorbed in the moment. Babaji said, "I have not had a bath to-day." Both Parmananda-ji and I were looking at him askance. Parmananda-ji had not asked him to perform *puja* – why was he volunteering this information as though a sin was about to be committed. Babaji had reached Paharpani from Haldwani at dawn, it was possible he had not bathed. However, I could not figure why it was so important.

Indicating the bathing place, Parmananda-ji said simply, "you can have a bath now".

Babaji gazed instead at the river flowing below the *ashram,* where on earlier occasions, too, he had taken a quick dip. He said "I want to bathe in the *sangam.* But they are burning their dead there. It may upset their sensibilities if I become an *avadhut* and *chita bhasma lepo.*" While the ash from cremation grounds is used in sacred worship by smearing on the naked body, these are practices that are not performed in a social setting, where they could have terrifying implications. Babaji was merely going to bathe in the river, so what on earth was he saying and why?

Parmananda-ji said, "You can bathe a little above the spot."

All the while, Babaji was running in and out of Parmananda-ji's room putting many layers of his clothes by, like a hyper-active child preparing for a cold bath. He emerged draped in his bathing *dhoti.* He then asked for a *lota.* Parmananda-ji pointed to a lota. Babaji said, "This *lota* is for children – I want a big one." And with that he made the old *sanyasin* go indoors to collect a suitable sized vessel with which he could pour water on himself.

Seemingly not satisfied with the commotion he was creating, he also tried to revive an earlier argument he had started about how many children so-and-so has, and which ones are alive and which dead – a subject of complete irrelevance to these two great *yogis.* Before Babaji left, just to add the additional garnish to the disturbance, he turned to me and said, "Now you can stop making angry faces at me, and instead make angry faces at Parmananda-ji."

With Babaji having left, Parmananda-ji returned to the conversation that was already there, waiting to be expressed. He spoke of the eternal Truth about which many books have been written, many terms used, great theories expounded, many techniques and practices perfected. In the time between Babaji leaving for a bath till he returned, Parmananda-ji spoke of the *Nada* with which I had been deeply absorbed in the morning. He took me through the different phases of realisation at the many levels of *samadhi.* We both traversed back easily and comfortably to the everyday world, immersed in a higher state of devotion.

A devotee of Parmananda-ji who was visiting him, sat all the while in total silence. I was not aware of him or of anything else. I wrote every word of what Parmananda-ji said because in it was the wisdom that is conveyed again and again by the great saints, and which like a meteorite through space, vanishes in the completion of its journey. Babaji returned from his bath and expressed the delight of both Hairakhandi Babaji and Sombari Babaji.

He said, "You can both speak in English, since I don't understand ABC. Have you been speaking in English?" I said, "I have not started speaking yet." Parmananda-ji replied that we spoke in... Surprisingly, while I remember everything else, I don't remember the words he used to convey the language spoken. Truly it is the eternal language of *yogis* – it transcends time and space, individual consciousness.

And what did he say, that so easily took me to the Highest Truth in *sahaj samadhi,* while still rooted to the ground? It has never mattered to me who these great *yogis* are, because I have known them only as Unified Consciousness. Yet people always ask, "who is he and how can I have his *darshan.*" So I am left to paint a factual picture of the person - the medium of the body through which that Truth was spoken. The answer to the question 'Can I have his *darshan*? '. Yes, you can see him, certainly. It must be rare in today's world to meet someone born in 1889, with his faculties so sharp that his physical age escapes notice. It must indeed be a blessing simply to meet him.

Swami Parmananda-ji took out his voter's card as proof of the birth I did not require, but was asking about in questioning a *yogi* of his pre-*sanyas* life. Born in Kashi on 10th October, 1889 into a Kashmiri Brahmin family which had migrated there many generations ago, his grand-father was a Bar-at-Law at the High Court. He himself spent his childhood in Assam, completing his school education at Shillong, before studying medicine from Nilratan Sarkar Medical College, Kolkata, at the time called Campbell College. His early service years as a physician were in the Eastern sector, both in Bengal and Assam. In fact, his spoken Hindi has a distinct Bengali *taan* or strain, that I had once commented on, and which had caused Babaji to tell him, "she will cook a Bengali meal for you".

Swami Parmanada-ji's initial meeting with his *guru maharaj*, Swami Vishuddhananda Puri was in 1933-34. In 1937, he took *sanyas diksha*. About the intervening years, Babaji enquired, "You came to the *sanyas ashram* from the *grihastha ashram*?" (You were a householder before taking *sanyas*?)

Parmananda-ji quibled back, "we are all born in the *grihastha ashram*." Babaji quickly agreed that apart from Lord Shiva Himself, certainly we are born of parents, and into the *grihastha ashram*, as part of the laws of creation.

Satisfied, Parmananda-ji replied to the question that Babaji had put on my behalf, "I lived in the world and participated in the usual process of living and earning, but I never married." Parmananda-ji had spent some 5-7 years of his *sanyas* life in *bhraman* as a wandering mendicant, he had spent two years at Rishikesh, 12-13 years in sadhana at Vrindavan *dham*, and some 30 years in this region of Kumaon. From 1990, he lives mostly at Sombari Babaji's *ashram* in Padampuri.

Sri Parmanandaji said, "In spiritual life, for a seeker of the Truth, for *atman gyan* or self realisation, for *tatwa-darshan* or transcending the elements of Earth, Water, Fire, Air and Space of which our gross bodies are composed, *guru diksha* or awakening by a *guru* is necessary.

"A *mantra* or name is given and *kapre* or the saffron cloth is given. The *sadhak/shishya* or spiritual practitioner/disciple is shown the expected behaviour that will form the lifestyle of the *marg* or path. With that, *japa* or *sadhana* of the *mantra* begins. When the *mantra* becomes *jagrat* or awakened, *diksha prakaran* happens, or the initiation into spiritual life. There are different processes through which this is done. On the *bhakti marg,* or path of devotion, *naam japa* is the fulcrum. *Yogic prakriya* or techniques of *yoga* are the process of purification on the *yoga* and *gyan margs.* Through this medium, *anahata nada* or the cosmic vibration that is within us and without us, which is the very basis of life, is awakened. *Anahata nada* or *kundalini* is awakened. At the time of awakening, the *guru's* help and guidance is needed. In such a state, the *shishya* keeps hearing the *nada* – it is sometimes in the sound of a *shankha* or *ghanta* – there are different *prakar* or kinds of *nada.* The *sadhak* cannot understand where the sound is from, he can become confused. The *guru* then directs his attention inwards. Within his *hridaya* or the *anahata chakra,* the *nada* resides. Here the *sadhak* comes face to face with his *ishta deva,* or personal deity.

"Within the *chida akasha* or space of undivided consciousness, the *nada* is left behind, and *jyoti* is awakened. The *jyoti* or light becomes *prakash* or the Light of Knowledge. Beyond the *jyoti,* the *suksham* or subtle realms are awakened. One becomes aware of *pitr-loka* and *deva-loka.* After this, comes *atman darshan* or self-realisation. Within *atman darshan* too, there are stages of realisation. When one realises the *Veda Vakya, Aham Brahmasmi,* I am That *Brahman,* there is still *ahankar* of *atman darshan.* Great saints like Vishwamitra and Durvasa have also acted from this *ahankar* before crossing the threshold beyond.

"After this stage one realises *Sarvam Khalvidam Brahman,* all is *Brahman,* there is nought but *Brahman.* When one is immersed in this state of consciousness, one becomes fully sacrificed, completely surrendered. One becomes like a child who will eat when fed, and sleep when put to sleep. But the mother allows the child to grow, and as he grows, her responsibility lessens. At this stage one has become *karma-tyagi, karma-vyaparit* – or beyond *karma. Karma atit ho gaye* – karma is now in the past. This is *sthitho pragyan avastha* – the state of Supreme consciousness. One no longer performs any personal work, one works for the welfare of creation, for God, for the welfare of the world. *Ek se prapti se jagat ki prapti,* from personal welfare to social welfare. The *gyan marg* involves *karma.* Without *karma,* we cannot live.

"Many remain in the state of duality, enjoying the bliss of *dvaita,* enjoying the *Bhagwat Lila* or Divine Play of Existence, and do not enter into the *ananda* of *nirvikalpa.* The *sadhak* who remains immersed in the *purnananda* of Consciousness, the Pure Bliss of Existence, does not return. Yet, only if he returns is this process possible."

Parmananda-ji smiled at me. I continued for him, "One enjoys the *lila* thereafter. Without the devotion of duality, *thair nahin payenge* - one will not be able to maintain the body." He nodded wordlessly.

Babaji returned from his bath in the *sangam* and announced that both Hairakhandi Babaji and Sombari Babaji were delighted. Babaji had not been physically present during our conversation, but as we left, Babaji acknowledged Parmananda-ji with, "I will call you Paramhamsa-ji" . There are different stages of *sanyas,* and other than the *avadhut* aspect, *Paramhamsa* is the highest stage, where neither good nor evil remain, all is One.

Parmananda-ji replied, "You can call me anything you like."

dhyana

CHAPTER 8

Siddhashram

ॐ

Bhawani Shankaro Bande
Shraddha Vishwas Rupenaon
Yabhyam Bina na Paschanti
Siddha Swanta Sthimiswaram

–Tulsidas' Ramayana

Salutations to Bhawani Shankar: Mata Parvati & Lord Shiva
Whose very attributes are shraddha and vishwas
Without whose grace
Siddhas themselves cannot be enlightened

After reaching *Siddhashram* at Sitlakhet, I spent the days in solitude and *dhyana* till *Janamashtami.* Several hours were spent alone at the small Shiva temple that Sri Hairakhandi Babaji had established.

The original *shakti* here, the Shiva *lingam* consecrated by Hairakhandi Babaji is not obviously visible. Another *lingam* appears to have been placed subsequently. He had also consecrated a *prateek* or symbol of Mata Vaishno Devi, so that villagers who could not go to distant Vaishno Devi in Jammu, could have the Devi's *darshan* here. Apparently, this is no longer here. The temple now has a small benevolent *murti* of Devi. A couple of other *murtis* are later additions. A relatively large *murti* of Hairakhandi Babaji sits in meditative posture. It would have been added subsequently. Looking up, the keystone to the dome is unmistakably familiar.

Someone has painted the beautiful natural stone inside the temple a plastic green. For convenience, a tap has been installed which drops water into the copper *kalash* on top of the Shiva *lingam*, against usual norms and aesthetics. The original stone slabs of the floor have been replaced with cement. As a later addition, a veranda surrounds the temple and at one side, before the entrance, a nook has been created where Hanuman-ji now stands in protection.

One can clearly envision the simple temple Hairakhandi Babaji had built to invoke sacred energies. The vibrations here remain potent and palpable, despite the attempts to modernise the temple, as is the trend at most old temples now. I learnt that there is an intention to replace the lovely stone slabs in the veranda outside, with marble. The architecture of an era reflects the sensibilities of a time. Today's temples are a reflection of the physicality of current existence and the premium on ostentation. Outside the temple, the *havana kund* remains witness to the changing times.

Sri Gorakh Babaji arrived here early on *Janmashtami* and began the day with a *havana*, maintaining an *akhand dhuna* for the 2 days of his visit. Above, the *shaktipeeth* of the region at the Syahi Devi *mandir* at nearly 9,000 feet stands in protection. Ahead is a vast valley, the ridge of Almora town, and the distant hills beyond. At the *havana kund* in front of Hairakhandi Babaji's temple at *Siddhashram* in the midst of forest cover, the *agni* or fire leapt to life. The *havana* was perfect and complete. I sat here many hours in *dhyana* with Babaji. In the evening, along with the *pujari* who looks after the temple and *ashram*, we commemorated the coming of Sri Krishna over 5000 years ago, in quiet celebration.

Early the following day, along with the *pujari*, we set off on foot for the Syahi Devi temple, 3-4 kms of an arduous climb away. Hariakhandi Babaji is supposed to have visited here before he settled awhile at Sitlakhet, establishing *Siddhashram*. The ancient temple is now in the midst of the dwelling places of the *pujaris* and their families who have grown to become an entire village. There is a poorly maintained Gorakhnath-ji *dhuna* at the entrance to the temple. Nearby, in a state of disrepair, is a Bhairav *mandir* with a *dhuna* within, as well as another *dhuna* outside. The Syahi Devi *mandir,* an ancient place of worship where several great saints, including Swami Vivekananda, have visited and done *tapasya,* has been ravaged by time. The Devi within the Syahi Devi temple remains untouched and remarkably serene and beautiful in her ancient form. Within her is the *shakti* to create again and to re-ignite the flame that smoulders here.

En route to the temple, at the few shops of Sitlakhet, Sri Gorakh Babaji stopped to chat with the small town's few people who had gathered to greet him. Among them was Narayan Dutt Pathak, the only remaining one of Siromani Pathak's six sons. Siromani Pathak was a devout and well-loved devotee of both Sri Hairakhandi Babaji and Sri Sombari Babaji. Narayan Pathak invited us to his home opposite the State Bank of India. He showed us the hand-written school copybook in which his father had written about Hairakhandi Babaji in a mixture of Hindi and Kumaoni, often with poetic eloquence. Another copy is filled with accounts about Sombari Babaji, which has been printed into a booklet. The late afternoon was spent in spontaneous *satsangha.* Sri Gorakh Babaji accepted Narayan Pathak's invitation for *prasad* the following morning.

The following day, after our morning *havana* we walked up to his house. His nephew, Guddu Pathak, read out from the ink-smeared yellowing pages of Siromani Pathak's copy about Hairakhandi Babaji. It was a treasure trove.

When Siromani was aged 13 or 14, Sri Hairakhandi Babaji who was travelling in a *doli* or palanquin, stopped outside their home and asked, "where is my devotee Siromani?" He was taken in to where the young boy lay, suffering excruciatingly from an infected boil. Babaji hugged him and took him in his lap. The young Siromani was cured. Everyone, particularly Siromani, requested Babaji to stay with them. He spent 3 days in the small dwelling place beneath the shop that Siromani tended.

At the insistent request of the villagers, Sri Hairakhandi Babaji agreed to stay at Sitlakhet. The villagers were eager to donate land for a proposed *kutia.* Babaji asked each to bring a *lota* or vessel of water from their property. When all the *lotas* were collected, there was one that consisted of a handful of water collected from the marshland, because there was no source of water there. When Babaji tasted it, he described it as *amrit* or the nectar of immortality, and asked to be shown the location. He indicated that this was where the *ashram* would be. Eventually Babaji spent three years here.

When Babaji said he would build his *kutia* on the land from where the sweet water came, it was pointed out that there was no source of water there. There are different versions of what happened thereafter, but essentially the *bhav* or essence of it is the same. According to the popular version, Babaji poked his forefinger into the earth and water sprang out. The more likely sequence of events, as gathered from different versions, is that he pointed with his forefinger and told his devotees this is where the water will come from. He sat in *dhyana* for 24 hours, performing *anushthan* or worship. The source of water was found. Even today, this is the source of the water here. The water is pure, refreshing and rejuvenating, as the Ganga is at its source. There is something almost tangibly sacred about it – one is compelled to remember that it was described as *amrit* by Sri Babaji.

At the time of Hairakhandi Babaji's visit, accompanying him was the lawyer, Bhola Dutt Pande, who was responsible for looking after *Siddhashram* till his death. After Pande died, Khimanand Pathak succeeded him as the *pujari.* Because of the consequent disarray, one of Narayan Dutt's brothers had requested Mouni Baba of Garsia near Ramanagar, to live here and manage the *ashram.* Later, because of conflicts between Pande's family and Mouni Baba, with both claiming rights, a protracted legal battle ensued and the land was divided between the two, with the *ashram* properties being divided and the *mula ashram* being given to the Trust formed by Mouni Baba. Before

Mouni Baba passed away, he willed the property to his faithful devotee, Pushkar Pathak. Between the temple and the two trees once planted by Hairakhandi Babaji, Mouni Baba's devotees have since built a marble lined hall to mark the *samadhis* of Mouni Baba and Shanta Mai, who lived here.

Bhole Baba or Balak Baba became well-known in the years between 1970 and 1984. He was hailed by new devotees as the re-appearance of Hairakhandi Babaji. All those whom I met who knew Hairakhandi Babaji had their reservations and were unable to accept Bhole Baba as the *mahatma* they had known. *Sants* in the *sadhu samaj* withhold comment on the matter. At Sitlakhet it is said that Bhole Baba came in a large convoy with great fanfare and held a *bhandara* here, which was taken as an indication of a bid to claim the *ashram.* Those who attended the *bhandara* say that Bhole Baba touched the food in blessing and said that it should be distributed as *prasad,* before he left.

At Kathgaria in Haldwani, the *pujari* spoke of Bhole Baba's visit there, and the inability of locals to accept it as the return of Hairakhandi Babaji. According to local reading, this is why Bhole Baba finally built an *ashram* at Chiluanaula near Ranikhet, instead of the s*haktipeeths* already established by Hairakhandi Babaji. At Hairakhan, across the river from where Hairakhandi Babaji spent considerable time in *tapasya* at the cave, Bhole Baba built an *ashram,* where his *samadhi* remains. Bhole Baba is known to have spent time in *tapasya* in this region.

It must be added that the acceptance or non-acceptance of Bhole Baba by Hairakhandi Babaji's original devotees who had spent time with him at close quarters, is not in itself a criteria of determination. A comment by Swami Brahmananda Puri, who has been staying at Ranibag for several years now and had also met Bhole Baba, deserves repetition, "Whoever he may have been, that he had *siddhis* and did much good work, is without doubt." Other *sadhus* have said, "Hairakhandi Babaji *ke gaddi pe baitha tha.* (He occupied the position).That alone is deserving of respect. Those sitting on the Shankaracharya's *gaddi* too are regarded as Shankaracharya, and in them vests the authority of the position."

At *Siddhashram* in Sitlakhet, with the passing years, the villagers stopped coming to pay their respects at the temple, because over time they were disillusioned that the *ashram* had lost its essence as Hairakhandi Babaji's *ashram* but had become Mouni Baba's *ashram* instead. Moreover, they were deeply resentful of the fact that Hairakhandi Babaji's *kutia*, where he had lived, was pulled down. The *sant kutia* which he had made for visiting saints, in which Sombari Babaji, Sitaram Babaji and other revered saints have stayed, is still in existence, but in a deplorably dilapidated state. On top of the *dharamshala* which Babaji had built for visiting guests, Mouni Baba's own dwelling place was built.

Where Babaji would do the sacred *panch agni tapasya* is also no longer discernible. *Panch agni* is a supremely sacred practice, which bestows immeasurable *shakti* or power. Hairakhandi Babaji was a *siddha* or adept of *panch agni* and was, on occasion, known to have taken *agni samadhi* during the *panch agni.* Those who witnessed it, or had heard about it from others who had, speak in awe and reverence about it. Other *sadhus* of the time, deeply influenced by it, were *sadhaks* of *panch agni*, which they learnt to practice under his guidance.

Possibly unintentionally, in the passing of hands, much that was sacred and immeasurably precious has been lost. Hidden is the immortal Babaji who inspired *Siddhashram*, a symbol of the loftiest aims, of the highest goals that man can strive for, while living in the world of men. Hairakhandi Babaji is not known through the five senses nor through the physical body of five elements, nor yet the mind that moves in ten directions. There are few places I have been more aware of *siddha-loka* than at *Siddhashram.* There is something perfect and whole, a sense of timelessness, the wonder and joy of eternity that is ever-present at *Siddhashram.* Hairakhandi Babaji reiterates through the yellowed pages of Siromani Pathak's writing, "Ultimately, the victory is of Truth."

Inspired by Sri Gorakh Babaji, Narayan Pathak came to the *ashram* after many years of having abandoned it. He was overcome with emotion for Hairakhandi Babaji, claiming he feels his presence here again. Sri Gorakh Babaji explained to him that no matter how aggrieved they are at the current situation, they must continue to visit the temple. He also promised to return here and have a *yagya* in which all the villagers can participate. Siromani's son Narayan said, "*Maharaj*, if you will live here awhile and build your *kutia*, I still have some land below the *ashram*." With folded hands he said, "Who knows what divine play is still waiting to unfold?"

Siddhashram is the fulcrum, it possibly holds the key to subsequent events. The days spent here were in an entirely different realm of timelessness, of perfection, of infinite possibilities. I began writing this book without planning it. I had intended to write about several Himalayan saints. I was already researching for a book, tentatively titled, *Shiva Darshan &Kailash Prakaran.* As I wrote, I realised this book is about Hairakhandi Babaji. I also realised that I was going on a pilgrimage to many different places with which he had been associated. Sri Gorakh Babaji said in passing, without a reference, "*Iske rahasya bahut gehra hai.*" The mystery of this is very deep. I agreed with him, aware then of what exactly it meant. Later, on the train from Lal Kuan to Mathura to visit Vrindavan, deeply aware that I was returning slowly to worldly spaces, I asked him what his statement had meant. Did I need the comfort of words to secure what I already knew? He laughed and said, "That floppy will not open here. It is connected with *Siddhashram*."

At *Siddhashram*, Hairakhandi Babaji is a living presence, more tangible and more real than flesh and blood. His presence is everywhere, within and without. I was in perfect tune with the timeless space of *siddhalok* where all things are not only possible, all thoughts are a reflection of what already is and what will be. My thoughts were not of this limited mind. The mind was so perfectly still, that the smallest vibration could be traced back to aeons of living and the ringing peals of an ever-widening circle could be heard till they faded into total silence. I could only hear the cosmic sound of being.

Such a state of perfection lived in total awareness is by the grace of those beings who live in higher realms. As we live in *bhu,* the world of everyday consciousness, we can enter the different *lokas* of *bhuvah, swah, maha, jana* and return with the experience, knowledge and wisdom of these realms. *Bhuvah* is the ancestral and intermediate realms, connected to our sub-conscious mind, known in our dream state, when the mind is still kriya-oriented. *Swah* is the celestial realms, of *devaloka,* of heaven, and is known unconsciously in our deep sleep state. Very close to heaven is hell, as reflected in our daily lives itself, where heaven and hell are states of mind in seamless transition. When we have exhausted our time in heaven earned from the merit of action, we must return to earth to pay our karmic debts. If this is done in supreme awareness, if all our actions are *nishkama,* or detached, we can cross the threshold again without suffering, piercing the veil of *maya* which causes us to believe that we are born and we die. To cross the threshold to *mahaloka* and *janaloka,* the realms of *siddhas* and of *rishis,* is by grace. This state is not attainable without *tapasya,* it cannot be maintained while retaining a sense of individual consciousness and the consequent *ahankar* which arises from it. To know this is through the grace of the eternal *siddhas* and *rishis* beyond birth and beyond death, through the grace of *Adi Siddha, Siddheswar* of *siddhas,* Bhagwan Shankar. *Tapahloka* is the eternal *samadhi* of Being, of Pure Consciousness. And there is *Satyalok.*

When it was time to leave *Siddhashram* on a perfect sunlit morning, as all the mornings before had been, I awoke with the awareness of dawning light and of the Himalayan skies through the window. I remained in meditation until I knew the sun would begin to rise across the hills. I folded my hands in acknowledgement of Surya Narayana, the witness of manifestation. I paid my respects at the *mandir* and the *havana kund,* through which direct knowledge is revealed. As we left, the invisible doors of *siddhalok* shut silently behind me again.

CHAPTER 9

Hairakhandi Babaji at Siddhashram

ॐ

Asato Ma Sadgamaya
Tamaso Ma Jyotir gamaya
Mrityorma Amritam gamaya
– Brhadaranyaka Upanishad — I.iii.28

From the Unreal lead me to the Real
From the darkness of Ignorance lead me to the Light of Knowledge
From Death lead me to Eternal Life

Siromani Pathak's hand-written copy of how *Siddhashram* came to be, brought alive the magic of a lost time. The players have all left the stage, but the essence of the tale remains, as it is in the epics. Through the pages of history we see the future unfold. Sri Gorakh Babaji often says, "He who does not know his history, jeopardises his future." Indeed the answers to the present lie in the causes of the past, just as today we write our future in indelible ink. He who knows the cause no longer grieves, he is forever freed. He can then complete the *karmic* debt of existence without becoming attached to the players or the play. He is no longer bound to the chain of time. He can enjoy the *lila,* for that is all it is.

Siromani, whose academic learning was limited to class 2, was moved to poetic form, even in the telling of ordinary events, writing vividly and eloquently for posterity, admitting that it was by the grace of Hari Dass Hairakhandi Babaji. At

Babaji's query to the villagers, "Who will give land?" Nar Dev Pathak, Siromani's father readily volunteered and along with Ratan Singh Routella, the *gram pradhan* or village head, organised the process of getting land from various villagers. Pandit Gauri Dutt Pant is also acknowledged in this context. Pandit Jwala Dutt Joshi, a lawyer, took an active part in the events that followed.

At the appropriate time, having sent word to Hairakhandi Babaji, who was at the time at Nainital, Babaji's devotee Bhola Dutt Pande, a lawyer by profession, arrived on horseback, *safa* or turban on head, and did *arati* of 'Sri Mahatma'. Referring to Hairakhandi Babaji, Siromani has used many epithets: Sri Swami Narayana, Hari Prabhu, Siddha Baba, Siddha Yogi, Sri Yogiraj, Sri Baba, 108 Sri.

Hairakhandi Babaji instructed them not to consider gain and loss, the water there is "*nirmal, amrit jaise,* (sweet like the sacred nectar of immortality), *siddhashram mein dhuni jalao*" (Light the *dhuni* at *Siddhashram*), thereby also indicating the name of the place. Babaji spoke of "*Bhagwati Ma Nirakar dhuni*" as "*Bhag-Bhagwan*", the eternal form of manifestation, which is essentially what *dhuni* worship is. Referring to Siromani as Sombari-ji's devotee, he advised him to shed all fear and go ahead with the work. Along with Bhola Dutt Pandey, they proceeded to organise the *bhumi ka benaama,* or registration of the land. Babaji's instructions were to give the rightful price to anyone who wanted to sell their land. However, everyone was happy to donate land for the building of *Siddhashram,* and the realisation of a noble dream.

Siromani Pathak particularly alludes to when Hairakhandi Babaji arrived and drank the water, and established *Siddhashram.* He consecrated a *murti* of Vaishno Devi. For twelve days, he did *agni-tap.* A *Ram Sahasranaam* was organised. *Yagya* and *anushthan* were performed, with *pandits* like Sri Yogendra and Sri Chandra Dutt participating. *Vidhwan* Narendra Dutt Shastri from far-off Kashi-Benaras, among others, was present. Bhola Dutt Pandey managed the organisational aspect.

The list of people who donated money and in kind, and by offering *seva* include Har Govind Ballabh Pant who became an M.P., the lawyer Govind Ballabh Pant father of politician K.C. Pant, Pandit Badri Dutt Tiwari of Tyonara, Saalam, Pandit Shiv Dutt Joshi and Gayatri Swarup, Devki Nandan Pande of Tarikhet, Pandit Govind Ballabh Joshi of Almora.

When it was proposed that the land should be in Hairakhandi Babaji's name, he protested saying, "Will you make of me a *grihastha* or householder, then?" He suggested that it be in Bhola Dutt Pande's name and that later a Trust be formed. Siromani Pathak readily agreed that Bhola Dutt was the obvious choice, capable of the responsibility thrust on him. Other than Bhola Dutt Pande, active participation was provided by Lala Radhe Shyam of Kashipur; Bishambar Pande; Lala Banwari Lal; Badri Dutt Joshi, a lawyer and Chariman of the Municipal Corporation; Vishnu Dutt Joshi of Salla Gaon; Shastri Manorath Pandey of Doongri, Saalam; and Siromani Pathak himself. The *sanyasin*, Anand Giri founded a school here.

Many of the people who joined forces were not only involved in spiritual work, they were deeply involved in the freedom struggle for which Babaji was a source of inspiration, as can be seen from the incident in Nainital when he lit his *dhuna* on Mall Road and challenged the separatist policy of British rule by which Indians were treated as inferior. In fact, veteran freedom fighters of the area took courage from Hairakhandi Babaji. India's independence, based on the principle of *dharma* or righteousness, was intrinsically connected with her spiritual might. In India's long and chequered history, there has always been the recognition of the contribution of the great *mahatmas* and saints.

When we stand at crossroads in our life, *dharma* or righteousness can become blurred and difficult to define. In the process of development and acquisition of wealth and power, *ahankar* or ego of personal power can become so marked, that we forget that the Law of Nature demands collective good and surrender to a Higher Power, if we are not to be destroyed in the process.

Our political history has always been connected with our spiritual strength. During the great wars of the *Ramayana* and the *Mahabharat,* Lord Vishnu himself came as the *avatars,* Sri Rama and Sri Krishna, to restore balance and values. It is the promise of the Scriptures that in every age, God Himself will come to restore this balance.

Hairakhandi Babaji reminded everyone not to become attached to the *ashram,* but to do *nishkama karmayoga,* or the selfless work of God. He also warned that anyone who does *chal-kapat,* or betrays trust will be destroyed. He said anyone who has *moha* or desire for the *ashram,* who eyes the *ashram* personally, '*hoge sarvanash unke, path narak jaane ka*' would be ruined for this is the road to hell. Furthermore indicating the future he said, Truth will be the ultimate victor, *Siddhashram* would be an *ashram* of *Dharma,* a shining light which would provide *prakash* or light and knowledge.

The Scriptures indicate the four *ashramas* or stages in life. *Brahmachari ashrama* is for the life of a student, the *grihastha ashrama* as a householder is intended to fulfil aspirations and desires, *vanaprastha ashrama* is for social retirement to cultivate devotion and one-pointedness towards God. *Sanyasa* is to discover the nature of the self, to know and live the Truth. These defined phases of life were in order to achieve the four goals of *artha, kaam, dharma* and *moksha.* Everyone went through this transition. It is sometimes suggested that because many people got involved in *artha* and *kaam* and lost the clarity to transit to later phases within the life cycle, some people renounced the world in order to focus on *dharma* and *moksha* and be able to develop techniques for balanced living for society. Such thinkers were known as *vidwans* and they devised the social code of conduct and the *Samkhya* philosophy.

Hairakhandi Babaji said, living in the *grihastha ashram,* or as a householder, *yoga* is possible, as the mute can speak with *kripa* or grace. Being at *Siddhashram*, allow your sins to be washed away. He indicated the natural way to do this, by following the law of *karma.* He said, let the wealthy donate in cash and kind, let *vidwans* or knowledge-holders teach, those who are in *vanprastha* should seek God, and *santon ko Siddhashram mein rehne ki agyan di* or he gave permission and direction for *sadhu-sants* to live here.

The caste system was based on particular natural dispositions that fulfil an individual's *samskaras* or the deep impressions on the mind screen caused by *karmas* according to the law of causation. Since the law of *karma* will extract fulfilment, Lord Krishna too had indicated to Sri Arjun, that fulfilling the law of *karma,* by performing *nishkama karmayoga,* or selfless action detached from desire for the fruit, be free of action while still in this body. Accordingly, Babaji indicated the means of purification by which we can overcome our *karmas.* He said, *Brahmins* should practice the *Vedas* and live on *dakshina* or the offerings made to them, *Kshatriyas* should focus on righteous living through the four stages of life, *Vaishyas* or the business classes and tradesmen should donate wealth, *Shudras* should perform *seva* or selfless service.

Inspired by Hairakhandi Babaji, whose words were printed and distributed titled '*Om Namoh Vasudevaya*', which Babaji was known to utter often, *Siddhashram* became a centre for *satsangh, bhajan* and *kirtan.* As stated by Pathak, *yatis, sanyasins, yogis, sants* and *mahatmas* came to add glory to the place. The wealthy and the landed gentry came. Political leaders and the educated came. And came his devotees, the simplest of the simple, for whom he was always one of them.

Siromani recorded Babaji's teachings to overcome *maya* or ignorance and delusion and reach *Hari Dham* or Eternal Life. These included donate for the good of all, participate in *satsangha,* speak the truth, take God's name, do good towards others, maintain simplicity in all aspects of life. He said, wealth is wasted unless it benefits the *suksham sharir,* essentially meaning that which impacts the gross is transient, use all your resources towards evolution of the spirit. He further said, when you take God's name, you earn merit in heaven.

Siromani Pathak wrote that talking about spiritual experiences is unwarranted, yet he would mention a couple of experiences, no more, for fear that else it would earn him wrath. Once in the winter months, he was outside in the snowfall at night with Hairakhandi Babaji. Babaji moved towards the east and vanished. A stunned and weeping Siromani pleaded, "bless me." Later, the village *pathwari* said, a *sepoy* had come that way who claimed he saw someone 7 feet tall, strong, like Bhairav, his face lustrous and illuminated in the dark night with *tejas* or spiritual energy. He saw him sitting by a waterfront at Reuni with many others. Siromani thought, this must be him, and accordingly sent someone to find out. The man returned with a message for Siromani, saying, "Stop crying and come here."

He wrote about another incident for the lesson that he learnt from it hoping that others too might benefit from his experience. Through it, Hairakhandi Babaji had given him *darshan*, revealing the Truth. One moonlit evening, while staying at *Siddhashram*, he went outside to go to the toilet. On the way, he encountered a snake with raised hood like Lord Vishnu's *chattrapati* or the ceremonial umbrella that protects him. He remembered hearing that he who bows before a hooded serpent earns wealth and status, name and fame. Checking his emotions and controlling the fears that threatened to overcome him, intent on the fulfilment of his desire, afraid yet of death, he prostrated himself beneath the hooded snake.

When he finally looked up, he found himself at the feet of Mahatma Hari Dass who was smiling. Hairakhandi Maharaj said: "The snake is not here. Arise, arise, Siromani. *Bhramh nahin karo*, do not get involved in false modifications of the mind. Know that this experience is the Truth. Walk on, this time will pass. Keep patience and believe in God. Death is only a change of clothes. He who remains immersed in God's name finds eternal life. Sombari is your protector, fear not. Remember what Sombari has taught you, do not debase yourself with lowly thoughts. Take the name of Vasudevaya. Why will you leave the *pucca* road for the *kaccha* – the sure-footed paved path for the muddy trail, the mature for the immature, the mango for the *babool* or thorny barren plant, the real for the unreal. If you put your mind to wealth, you will have lost this time. Wealth prevents *bhajan* or putting your mind and energy one-pointedly to devotion. With wealth comes *lobh* or greed, and greed brings *moha* or desire and attachment. With *moha* comes tears of grief."

Siromani started weeping, and through his tears he said, "So long have I been sleeping. You have woken me from this deep sleep."

bhraman

CHAPTER 10

Golju & the Panchnama Devas

ॐ

Sanyasaha Karma Yogash cha Nihsresha Kara Ubhao
–Bhagwad Gita 5.2

Sanyas and Karma Yoga are both superior paths

The days of stillness and quietude in *sadhana* at Sitlakhet were followed by a period of *bhraman* or travel. Around Ranikhet some of the many places visited are all inextricably inter-woven with the culture, folklore and heritage of Kumaon that Hairakhandi Babaji was keenly familiar with, and which were the backdrop of his human existence.

Leaving Sitlakhet behind, a few kms from Kathpuria an old temple caught the eye, and we stopped to pay our respects to Golju Bhagwan. I was already familiar with Golju and the deep and abiding respect Kumaonis have for this particular aspect of the divine. Throughout Kumaon, many villages have a temple and *dhuna* dedicated to Golju. The main temple of Golju is at Champavat, while a large temple is at Chitai on the outskirts of Almora, a small temple is at Binayak near Bhimtal, and there is a *shaktipeeth* at Ghorakhal where Golju is believed to have done *tapasya.* There is a *tapasya dhuna* revered as a thousand year old *siddha dhuna* at Sunkungarh in Granao. Hairakhandi Babaji had done *tapasya* at all of these places.

The history and tradition of Kumaon accords great respect to Golju, a king of the Katyur dynasty, whose birth itself was a reflection of divinity. While he is included among the *Panchnama devas* of Kumaon, the *Panchnama devas* are regarded as his maternal uncles. He is the deity of the region, respected as the king and ruler, patron saint and protector. He is known by several names: Gorril, Golju, Golu, Goyal, Gajar, all of which relate to the same source. Gorril Deva is also regarded as Gaur Bhairav.

Harjyu, Shyamjyu, Airi Deva, and other *devas* of Kumaon are regarded as part of the *Panchnama devas*, and are associated with Vyana Dhura, some 25 kms from Tanakpur, through Sukha Dham. Another route leads from Champavat through a mountain trail to Tanakpur and onto Vyana Dhura. The *guru* of the *Panchnama devas* is Mahayogi Shiva-Goraksha. They are believed to be *siddhas*, as well as *deva-swarup*, or having attained to *devaloka*. Some among them were also kings.

Folklore states that Maharaja Jhalorai, called Kumaon Rajan, had seven queens, who had not conceived. At an advanced age, he married Kalinka, regarded as sister of the *Panchnama deva* and a form of Kali. When she was expecting a baby, the other queens felt belittled by their barren status. During her confinement, the co-wives took her to Dhumakot in Champavat and made devious plans to get rid of the newborn baby, heir to the throne.

Accordingly, they blindfolded Kalinka and removed a stone slab from the flooring of her dwelling place, from where the newborn was thrown down into the fodder in the cattleshed below, expecting that he would be trampled to death and devoured there. In place of the child, they put a *lohria* or rock. They informed the king that Kalinka had delivered this rock.

After a few days, when the queens checked in the cattle shed they found the young boy, Bala Goria, riding a goat, happily. They now devised a plan by which he was put in a cage and the cage was put into the dung heap. After several days, the boy was found still alive. Thereafter they put the cage into the river, where instead of going downstream, it is said to have moved upstream towards the *sangam* of Gauri and Kali-Sarda, ahead of Jauljibi. This is where Hairakhandi Babaji was last seen after his visit to Askot, from where it is believed he became *antardhyani* and dissolved his physical form.

A fisherman caught Golju in his extended net and took him home to his childless wife who was delighted, but expressed anxiety on how to feed him, because their single cow was without milk. It is said that the cow started giving milk and the foster mother of Gorril also had milk in her breasts.

One day, as the young child grew, the lad was playing with his wooden horse which legend claims could fly. To quench his thirst he went to the *naula* or source of water near the fortress at Champavat with his wooden playmate. The king, with his queens, was present there. The king's horse proceeded to the source of water. Gorril was asked to make way, but refused saying that his wooden horse would drink first. The queens mocked him asking, "since when did a wooden horse drink water?"

Gorril replied, "in a kingdom where the queen gives birth to a rock, a wooden horse can also drink water."

Hearing this, the king called the boy and demanded to be told the meaning of the statement. Upon hearing the entire story from the boy, he demanded proof of Gorril's claim. Gorril is believed to have said that milk from his rightful mother would reach his mouth as proof.

Satisfied by the proof, the king now decreed that the seven queens who had tried to kill the heir to the throne would be sentenced to death. Gorril pleaded mercy on their behalf and gained pardon for their lives. Later, the boy became a valiant king, known throughout the kingdom for his righteous rule. He created *panchayats* to facilitate the process of justice. Even today, the people of Kumaon go to Gorril Deva, both for justice and for clemency, as well as for blessings at the beginning of a new venture or an auspicious event.

Having lived in the region, I had often witnessed the

abiding faith in Golju Bhagwan. Grooms and brides dressed in their wedding finery seek Golju's blessings. A newborn is taken to the temple for his first outing. Even a new vehicle is first taken to the *mandir* for Golju's approval. Graduation, a first job, and all the times of joy are shared with Golju. Equally, before going to war, Kumaonis first seek the blessings of Golju, as some of the inscribed bells bear witness. The most touching incident I have seen is when a lady in the throes of a schizophrenic episode desperately sought to ride the time by pleading in surrender, *"Golju, tera haal chor diya."* Golju, a vibrant living energy, is part of the collective consciousness of Kumaon.

Chapter 11

Reuni Gufa, Jheula Devi

ॐ

Naam rattan kyon chora diya, naam rattan kyon chor diya
Maya ko to khub sajaya, naam rattan kyon chor diya
Naam japan kyon chor diya re...
Dhan-daulat ko khub sajaya, naam rattan kyon chor diya
Tu ne naam japan kyon chor diya
Kaam na chora, krodh na chora
Sat vachan kyon chor diya
Tu ne Lal Ratan kyon chor diya
Tu ne naam rattan kyon chor diya...

—*Bhajan of sadhus*

Why do you no longer take my name?
Resplendent is Maya - the veil of illusion,
Forgotten is the gem of my name
Wealth and prosperity placed on a pedestal,
Praise of me forsaken.
You have not abandoned desire, nor anger,
Why have you forgotten the Truth
Why did you forsake the true gem,
Why have you forgotten my name?

Without a specific itinerary and schedule in mind, we travelled at an unhurried pace. Along the way, we stopped at the various places associated with Sri Hairakhandi Babaji.

Reuni Gufa, Majhkhali

Few kms from the Golju *mandir* near Kathpuria, we reached Majhkhali. Some twenty years ago when I had first visited, it barely merited mention in a map of Kumaon. A century ago, it was in the midst of forests. Now the village of Majhkhali has spread into the flat lands, easy to terrace and cultivate. We walked along a narrow untidy trail between Himalayan village homes that have grown haphazardly over time.

At one place along the trail, Sri Gorakh Babaji stopped to cut the bramble and bushes by flaying his stick. There was nothing to indicate the *gufa* going into the bowels of the earth. Above it grew long wild grass, the opening was hidden by bramble. As the city-scrapers escape the attention of the subtle inner vision of a *tapaswi yogi*, the sacred hidden *gufas* of the Himalayas remain invisible to the gross vision of today.

Soon the opening to the *gufa* became visible. Hairakhandi Babaji is believed to have mentioned to Siromani Pathak, as recorded in his hand-written manuscript, that he spent twelve years in *tapasya* at the Reuni *gufa*, accompanied by another *sadhu*, with whom he lost touch thereafter. Sri Gorakh Babaji continued to clear the brambles before stepping inside this ancient *tapasya sthal* where Hairakhandi Babaji had done *tapasya* for twelve long years – a lifetime, indeed. As Sri Gorakh Babaji lit *agarbatti* or incense sticks, the flame leapt up with a will of its own. He sat awhile in the anterior of the cave, later remarking on the strong undisturbed vibrations within. Then he moved deep into the *gufa*. Soon he was standing full-length as the *gufa* broadened.

At the *havana kund* at *Siddhashram*, too, when Babaji held a lit stick to the damp wood of branches soaked by the monsoon downpours, in the absence of camphor or any other readily inflammable material, the flame danced high into the mountain air as though rejoicing it's very nature by which the gross transforms to the subtle, by which the gods themselves are appeased through *agni*, the celestial flame. It must be added here that Sri Gorakh Babaji is an adept of *dhuna vidya*, including *panch agni*, *jal havana* and other esoteric practices. I have witnessed the divine nature of *agni*, time and time again.

A few days later, at the *kutia* of Hairakhandi Babaji's

devotee, the late Guman Singh Naula, when Sri Gorakh Babaji lit the *diya,* there was a visible *jyoti,* or light, which extended along the *chimta,* witnessed by all three of us who were present: Sri Gorakh Babaji, Naula's grandson Kishen Singh, and I. Decades ago, when Siromani Pathak had seen lights near *Siddhashram,* Hairakhandi Babaji had explained that being a sacred place, *siddhas* sometimes visit. These lights have been reported at other *siddha sthans* I have visited, like Rudranath and Chandrashila above Tungnath among the Panch Kedar in Garhwal, both places of *tapasya* where Hairakhandi Babaji has visited. Sri Gorakh Babaji and other *yogis,* as well as the temple *pujaris* who maintain strict austerities during the months they are responsible for conducting worship at these temples, have all confirmed my own experiences and impressions of many of these remote sacred places.

Siddheshwar Mandir

Years ago, there was no metalled road in this area. On a trail in the dense forests, Hairakhandi Babaji, the wandering mendicant, went from one sacred place to another, oftentimes with other *sadhus* like Sombari Babaji, Laturia Babaji, Jangam Babaji, Sitaram Babaji. He graced many *tapasya sthals* with his presence, keeping the flame of *tapasya* burning bright for *sadhaks,* whom he continues to inspire even today. There are many places where he built small temples, his *dhunas* still retain the energies that he awakened through them. In the many *gufas* where he sat absorbed in cosmic contemplation, the very rock itself retains the vibration of his being.

The *mula mandir* or main ancient temple at Siddheshwar *mandir* between Majhkhali and Ranikhet, has a natural Shiva *lingam,* powerful to behold, beneath a tree which now exists only as a stump. Around it, as is the fashion now, progress is being measured by increased construction.

Jheula Devi Mandir

At the edge of Chaubatia, Ranikhet, the Jheula Devi *mandir* is well known locally. Legend states that some 700 years ago, troubled by the leopards of Kumaon which took away their cattle and livestock, the villagers of this area were at their wits end. One night one of the shepherds dreamt that Ma Durga was indicating a particular place where a *murti* that had been worshipped in older times, lay below the earth. In his dream he was instructed that if a temple was built and consecrated to her, their troubles would come to an end. Accordingly, this was done and the area has since been protected by her. Later still, it is said, that the goddess wanted a *jheula* or swing and accordingly she was seated on it and became known as Jheula Devi.

The many bells that adorn the precincts of the temple are witness to the many hopes and dreams of devotees, their faith and their gratitude. Walking into the temple, clearly visible, was a beautifully sculpted idol of the Devi occupying centre stage, with a couple of other idols also receiving due attention. Not seeing any ancient *murti* and not being able to detect the source of the *shakti,* enquiry revealed that the original Devi has been relegated to a forgotten window The *pujari* explained that more beautiful *murtis* have replaced her. Sri Gorakh Babaji's only comment was, "*Yehi Kali Yug ka prabhav hai*" (This is the influence of the Kali Yuga).

Everywhere, the *shakti* of ancient temples and *tapasya sthals* are being ignored, and people are deluded into thinking that superficial form is true worth. Polished marble, granite and tiles are replacing stone and earth, as though man's limited creation has more worth than Nature's bounty. It is a sign of the times that the ancient temples are being pulled down to replace them with cold marble and the glitter of gold. These are the signs of *Kali Yuga* – when man is completely unaware of the existence of the subtle, when he can no longer discriminate between the real and the illusion, when *shakti* is thought to mean the power that money buys.

When we no longer value merit, it cannot accrue to us. The very earth hides her chosen ones. Like a seed that remains dormant, the *shakti* of the sacred remains hidden to manifest again when, with true devotion, her *darshan* is sought.

The people will soon wonder why Ma Durga did not fulfil her promise, as they continue to worship cold stone without *prana* or life energy in it. We have grown accustomed to mere lip-service, and so think that a perfunctory ritual can consecrate an idol. Only he who can invoke the gods has the *shakti* to consecrate a temple and infuse *prana* or living energy to a *murti.* He who has not the blessing of the gods cannot be a medium of blessing.

From the Jheula Devi *mandir,* it is said that there is an entrance to a nearby *gufa* where Hairakhandi Babaji had done *tapasya.* The ancient *gufa* has since been converted into a room, usually kept locked. While it was still an open cave, Sri Gorakh Babaji had spent a few days in *tapasya* here. Near the cave, Mouni Babaji, a Vaishnav *sadhu,* has built a Sri Ram *mandir,* an *ashram,* and a Sanskrit *vidyalaya* with some 65 residential students. Sri Mouni Babaji invited Sri Gorakh Babaji to stay at the *gufa.*

That evening we stayed at Ranikhet with a devotee of Babaji, a state minister. Their family put all else aside to do *seva* for their honoured guest, accompanied us to Chiluanaula, and spent the evening in quiet prayer and *bhajan.*

Chiluanaula

I was visiting Chiluanaula for the second time. The first time was barely months after Bhole Baba had passed away in tragic circumstances. As elsewhere, the place has expanded. It is well-maintained but there is something missing. Many *ashrams* have been handed down to coming generations without the continuation of a spiritual tradition. Many have grown wealthier, expanded, become more organised with a growing congregation. None of this has anything to do with spiritual tradition or the transmission of spiritual energy. At the gross level, as in the dynasty of kings, a weak link will ultimately create the downfall of the kingdom.

Well-known sages and masters who have built organisations

and empires are aware that it is a temporary phenomenon. Everything is transient, form is ordained to change. In the spiritual tradition, the lineage through which spiritual knowledge is conveyed is exacting in the extreme. With the passing of time, when particular traditions fade, it is the *rishis* and the *sia* who revive them again, re-connecting them with the original lineage, unborn and undying, where the *guru* is eternal, the *guru* is Sadashiva.

Sri Gorakh Babaji often says, in the account books of God, your palaces and your cars, your name and your fame will not be recorded, that you will have to leave behind in *mrityuloka*, the realm of Birth and Death. Only Truth is recognised there, nought else. All the merit you have acquired will earn you *bhog*, but it cannot earn you eternity.

Binsar Mahadeva

The morning found us beyond Tarikhet, in the midst of tall pine trees, blue skies and wispy cloud formations. Binsar Mahadeva is an ancient temple and *tapasya sthal*, that has changed its outer face according to the times we live in. There is a Sanskrit *vidyalaya*, where *Vedic* traditions are taught. The *sadhus* who live here have continued to uphold the age-old traditions. Here, too, Sri Hairakhandi Babaji and other great *tapaswis* have done *sadhana*. An old photograph of Hairakhandi Babaji, rarely seen, occupies pride of place near the *dhuna* in the *sant kutir*.

Neat and clean, there is a *gurukul* where the old and the new have compromised comfortably without loss of identity. I could not recall having been here before, yet there was something strangely familiar and yet completely unknown about the temple and *ashram* complex. Sri Gorakh Babaji, who had last visited here several years ago, expressed the sentiment, "I feel I just stepped into an old dream and I cannot recognise it anymore, but I do know it, certainly."

Gorakh Babaji on Janmashtami at Siddhashram, Sitlakhet

Gorakh Babaji at Reuni Gufa, Majhkhali

Airawat Gufa at Jageshwar

Chapter 12

Almora & Jageshwar

ॐ

Ya Devi sarva bhutesu Matri rupena samsthita
Ya Devi sarva bhutesu Shakti rupena samsthita
Ya Devi sarva bhutesu Buddhi rupena samsthita
Ya Devi sarva bhutesu Laxmi rupena samsthita
Namestasyai Namestasyai Namestasyai Namo Namaha

– *Durga Sapt Shati*

Praise be to the Divine Goddess in the form of the Universal Mother
Hail Ye who Art Energy Incarnate in all Existence
Thou who Art Discrimination, Knowledge and Wisdom in all Beings
Goddess of Plenty and Well-being in all Creation
Praise be to you! Again and yet again.

All the roads leading to Almora are immeasurably familiar. I return here as one who returns home. That I came as a stranger more than two decades ago, and lived three perfect years here, cannot explain the connections that bind me to the Kumaon Himalayas.

Khairnar

From Ranikhet, winding our way towards the plains, we visited Sombari Babaji's *tapasya sthal* near Khairnar bridge, across the river from a *mandir*. Though a road now runs adjacent to the *gufa*, which is consequently well-visited, it still reverberates with the energy of the *tapasya* done here. On the other side of the river, the *mandir* is an old *shaktipeeth* of Kali and of Bhairav. The idol of Kali here is a recent addition. Near the *mandir,* the surroundings have grown dirtier and more run-down, but the vibrations remain undisturbed, easy to re-awaken again.

Hairakhandi Babaji would visit here frequently on his travels to Nainital and Khurpatal via Ratighat. He would visit different *tapasya sthals,* guiding and blessing *sadhaks.* Even today, *sadhaks* in intense sadhana are aware of his presence. Many *sadhaks* have been keenly aware of his blessings as they crossed through particularly turbulent states, unknown and unfamiliar.

Kakrighat

Kakrighat, across the river on the main road to Almora, is an oft-visited familiar place for me. Over the years I have known many *sadhus* who have spent time here in *sadhana.* It is well known that Swami Vivekananda spent a night here. Conversations with local residents suggest that it is likely that he met Hairakhandi Babaji or Sombari Babaji, or both.

At Kakrighat, there is a living *samadhi* of Dev Puri, from some couple of centuries ago. *Raja* Devi Chand used to visit the *siddha sant,* Dev Puri, who regarded him as a *dharma bhai* or spiritual brother. Once when the *raja* came, Dev Puri told him to stay on here and not to proceed towards the jungle of Kala Dhungi, towards Kotabagh, where the kings of the region would customarily spend some of the winter months. He seemed willing to stay, but eventually, persuaded by one of his advisors, he proceeded on and was later killed by him, though he claimed the king had died of a snake bite. Even before news of this reached him, Dev Puri announced the king's death and his own intention of taking live *samadhi* for which he had a pit dug.

Here, Hairakhandi Babaji had done *tapasya* near the *mandir* and had also held *yagya, anushthan* and *bhandara.* Later, Sombari Babaji did *tapasya* beneath the *bat vriksha* or banyan tree. Hairakhandi Babaji's visits here were frequent. There are many tales regarding him and Sombari Babaji centred here. Several years of their lives coincided and they often travelled together, worshipped together during *yagyas* and *anusthan,* and visited each other. Hairakhandi Babaji retained utmost simplicity, preferring to remain unknown and usually remaining in the background, referring people to Sombari Babaji. When Hairakhandi Babaji would enter, Sombari Babaji would rise to welcome him and offer an *asana* as though Narayana himself had arrived. Devotees who witnessed Sombari Babaji's deep and abiding respect for Hairakhandi Babaji were often left wondering who the great saint could be.

Sombari Babaji was born into an established well-to-do Brahmin family of Punjab. After his mother died at an early age, he was cosseted by his *masi,* or mother's sister and their entire family. He showed early signs of walking the spiritual path and at the age of ten, he had already renounced the world. Much later, as it happened, he was at Badrinath when his father passed away and he performed the *antim samskaras* with traditional rites.

Sombari Babaji was a familiar figure in the Kumaon and Garhwal hills where he wandered, often with Hairakhandi Babaji. His chief *tapasya sthals* were at Kakrighat and Padampuri. He became known as Sombari Baba because of the *bhandara* he would host on Sombar or Mondays.

There is a story told of how a basket of *langra* mangoes came as *dakshina* for Sombari Babaji when he was at Kakrighat. He distributed one each to all around, despite the fact that the number of people were three times the number of mangoes. He gave 2 mangoes to a particular *sadhak* telling him to give the larger one to another *sadhu* some way across. Exchanging his own smaller mango for the larger one, the *sadhak* bit into it. His mouth filled with worms, which he was not able to get rid of. He was told to beg pardon of Sombari Babaji, who told him, "in future be happy with what is assigned to you. Do not covet what rightfully belongs to another." He explained that just taking the name of God is not enough unless one purifies oneself in thought and action. He said this should be a lesson to all those who had witnessed the incident.

Almora

Almora is the old capital and the epicentre of Kumaoni culture. The spiritual way of life and the inherent value systems that they bring to the fore have been an integral part of life here. Times are changing. Environmental pollution spares none. Merely two decades ago, Almora stood firm against the onslaught of decaying spiritual traditions. Even today, the glimmer cf the past remains like a spluttering light. Almora was never a tourist destination – the tourist traffic bypassed it, and the people of Almora were happy to be spared. I recall witnessing an incident at a shop, which was typical of the ethos of the place. A tourist walked in and asked the shopkeeper, "What can I buy here to take back as a souvenir?"

The shopkeeper's curt reply, "You cannot buy what there is plenty of here – peace."

Over five thousand years ago, the *Pandavas* are believed to have been here. Close to Almora, Katarmal has a fortress of the Katyuri dynasty where the kings have lived. Here there is a rare Surya *mandir*, in partial ruin, set atop the hill, in splendid solitude.

Hairakhandi Babaji had stayed in several places of this ancient town where the footprints of great sages remain embedded in the hearts of the people. In Almora, Nanda Devi is worshipped in remembrance. Nanda Devi, the *ishtha* Devi of Uttarakhand is none other than the daughter of Himavat - Uma-Parvati, Bhawani Shankar. Her temples are everywhere in Kumaon and Garhwal.

Hairakhandi Babaji is known to have stayed at Chitai, on the outskirts of Almora. The thousands of brass bells of all shapes, sizes and peals at the Golju *mandir* at Chitai, is the very symbol of worship of Golju's devotees, offered in deep faith and conviction. Golju stands witness in protection of his people.

Hairakhandi Babaji would also visit the Vishwanath *mandir* beside the gentle dancing Kosi river, as well as Patal Devi where Anandomayee Ma's *ashram* has since been established.

Anandomayee Ma had undertaken the Kailash *yatra* around 1940, and had mentioned that she had Babaji's *darshan,* believed to be near Milarepa's *gufa,* which is situated a little way up from the trail on the third day of the *parikrama* of Manasarovar Kailash. Hairakhandi Babaji had stayed at this *gufa* as well as at another *gufa* in the vicinity.

The Kasar Devi *gufa* and *mandir* is set atop a hill within Almora, but remains undisturbed by the expanding city. On his way to Jageshwar and Bageshwar, Babaji had done *tapasya* here, in the midst of forests, spending considerable time absorbed in contemplation. The energy here is palpable: the rocks, the wind, the very air itself, vibrates in intense meditation.

Swami Vivekananda had done *tapasya* at Kasar Devi. His spiritual experiences here and at Kakrighat are recorded. It is said that his original diaries have a wealth of information of this period of *sadhana* here and elsewhere. The volumes of published material are selected and edited versions of these diaries. It is conjectured that his experiences near Almora may have included a meeting with Hairakhandi Babaji.

Lama Angarika Govinda, a Tibetan Buddhist monk of German descent, an erudite scholar and author of *The Way of the White Clouds* and *Foundations of Tibetan Mysticism,* among other books, lived three decades near Kasar Devi. He has been known to have mentioned that he had met Hairakhandi Babaji.

Babaji was also affectionately called Lama Baba in Tibet, during the time he had helped several Buddhist *sadhaks.* He would habitually wear the robes associated with Tibetan Buddhist monks. He is believed to have also visited Lhasa and surrounding areas. It is said that Hairakhandi Babaji had altercations with some lamas who practiced human sacrifice.

Hairakhandi Babaji is known to have stayed at the Nanda Devi *mandir* in Almora. In Lala Bazaar, Babaji stayed at the Ram Mandir. He visited and probably also stayed at various *kulin* or aristocratic families of Almora, where he is still remembered through the generations.

On the road to Bageshwar, at the village of Gairar, a Rajput of over hundred years, used to recall anecdotes of Hairakhandi Babaji and Sombari Babaji. He said that he had met Hairakhandi Babaji at the *dhuna* of Golu Deva in the village of Gairar, beyond Joshi Gaon and Bhatt Gaon, where Hairakhandi Babaji is known to have stayed. He claimed that Babaji could use a *talwar* or sword with both hands, and would sometimes be seen with a *dhanush baan* from which fire would emanate when he shot an arrow.

Near Almora, on the road to Jageshwar, Hairakhandi Babaji stayed at Sakteshwar, close to Bare China. Near the bus-stop, he stayed at a *kutia* in the compound of Badreshwar Mahadeva, which had been established by someone who was blessed with a son after his visit to Badrinath. Later, Sombari Babaji also stayed here. Mahadeva Giri, among other saints, have also spent time here.

In the early 80's when we lived at Almora, it was natural that passing *sadhus* on their way to the higher Himalayas, or to and from their *tapasya sthals* would visit our home. The many renunciates living nearby were regular visitors. I realise now that it was an unusual occurence. At the time, I accepted their blessings with the same natural spontaniety with which they were given.

Jageshwar

Some 30 kms from Almora, beyond Bare China, the temple complex of Jageshwar is in the midst of a forest of *devadar* trees. It is a sacred place associated with Lord Shiva, regarded as foremost among *shaktipeeths*, and spiritually connected to the 12 *jyotirlingas*. Some people suggest that *'Nageshwam Dwaruka Bane'* in reference to the *jyotirlingas* actually indicates Jageshwar. The many ancient temples here are a reflection of a past era when this place is believed to have been among the *gupt* or sacred secret *tapasya sthals* in the Himalayas.

My visits to Jageshwar have spanned many years and have been associated with several people with whom I share a spiritual connection. Yet, Jageshwar has always been a scrapbook of distinct memories that stand stark without a reference, as though it was only an energy I had known and the physical manifestation was a mere dream. Jageshwar is the manifestation of *Shaivi maya*, which can sway all beings. It is also the ultimate transcendental experience for one without fear, who walks on faith alone, with total surrender.

The place was called Yageshwar from the time when the *sapt rishis* had done a major *yagya* here. It is also known as Jaganath. Nearby, *uttarbahani* and *purvabahini* rivers flowing north and eastwards, have their *sangam* or confluence. The waters are considered to be as sacred as the Ganga. As at Badrinath, the Brahma Kapali Brahma Kund is regarded as particularly auspicious for bathing.

The place merits mention in the *Manas Khand* of *Skanda Purana.* It is believed that Lord Shiva himself had done *tapasya* at Jageshwar for untold years and consequently all the gods and goddesses have done *tapasya* here, making it a place of powerful divine energies. It is referred to as Rikheshwar, where *rishis* have done *tapasya.*

The main temples in the complex here are of Jaganath, Mahamrityunjaya, Pushti Mata, Kedarnath, Naun Durga, Sri Hanuman, Pashupatinath and Surya *adi* Naun Graha. Many of the temples were built during the Katyur dyasty and also the Chand dynasty. According to tradition, the kings donated generously in the name of Jaganath, and some 365 villages were donated to the temple.The Kings are also believed to have kept their wealth here for safe-keeping, taking it at times of need. It is said that during the rule of Raja Deep Chand, a planned enemy attempt to capture the temple was successfully fobbed by a swarm of bees from Jhakar Sain which attacked the approaching army. It is well known that *siddha sthans* are protected by the unseen hand of divine providence.

The imposing and spectacularly large *devadar* tree at one end of the complex is believed to be some 5,000 years old. At the entrance is a Bhairav *mandir.* On the opposite side, there is also a *sanyasin dhuna.* Behind the Jaganath temple, within the complex is the living *siddha samadhi* of a Puri *sanyasin,* where *bhog* is offered, as at the temples in the complex. Across the river is a temple dedicated to Kuber, the god of wealth.

Among the many sacred places here are Jhakar Sain where there is a Shiva *lingam,* that arose when the *sapt rishis* witnessed Lord Shiva's divine *lila* and become aware of his *maya.* The Airawat *gufa,* where many *rishis* and *siddhas* have done *tapasya* is believed to have been from the time that Devaraj Indra, ruler of the celestial regions had disembarked here from his *vahan* or vehicle, Airawat. The divine elephant was among the precious *navaratna* which came from the ocean at the time of the great churning of the oceans.

This sacred *gufa* was a place of intense *sadhana* of Hairakhandi Babaji and other *siddhas* and *rishis.* In more recent times, Dhaula Devi's *tapaswi yogi* Bramacharya-ji, a well-known *sant* of Kumaon, had done *sadhana* here. In his childhood, he had been blessed by *darshan* of Hairakhandi Babaji between the years of 1915 and 1920. Dhaula Devi, some 10 kms away, is among the 108 *shaktipeeths.* Gyan Giri-ji, another well-respected saint of Kumaon had also done *tapasya* here. Sitaram Babaji, some 110 years old, who lives at Bridh Jageshwar, is among the many saints who have done *tapasya* here.

Sri Gorakh Babaji continues to maintain the ancient traditions during his frequent visits, in his continued pursuit to keep alive the tradition of *tapasya* in the *gufas,* which are increasingly becoming polluted and unsafe. It must be recognised that the Himalayan spiritual traditions are connected to the *gufas,* the forests and the sacred Himalayan mountains. It is imperative that the sanctity and purity of these are maintained, that they are kept protected and safe from vandalism as well as environmental and social pollution and that, as always, *sadhu sanyasins* are able to live in solitude in the *gufas.*

Tapaswi yogis have always lived in austere solitude and harnessed those energies that will bring peace, joy and wisdom to mankind. Spiritual thought and energy is deeply connected to the continuity of the *sadhu-sant-sanyas* traditions. They are the medium through which spiritual wisdom has always been, and continues to be, conveyed and revealed to mankind.

The ancient *tapasya sthals* in the mountains, forests and beside rivers, the *gufas* and *mandirs* need protection to continue a living tradition that is more threatened today than it has ever been. Protection of these sacred places is not by declaring them as historical monuments, bringing them under administrative supervision and highlighting them as toursit destinations, but preserving their original identity as places of worship of the Supreme Being. It is imperative that we maintain abiding respect towards what we have worshipped since time began: the earth, the rivers, the mountains, the natural environment.

In this age of unparalleled scientific progress, as we endeavour for material welfare and physical comforts, we need to preserve our ancient heritage and spiritual traditions if we are to enjoy an era of balanced growth and development. If the traditions of thousands of years that have stood the test of time are overthrown in arrogance, greed and ignorance, we would have done incalculable damage to humanity, to the Earth that has sustained us, and to all living beings.

From age to age, saints have kept alive universal values enshrined through their lives of truth, simplicity and love. It is these values that man has always aspired towards as the highest loftiest aims. May we continue to pay tribute to these ideals and the rare few who continue to be the living embodiment of an eternal tradition.

CHAPTER 13

Bageshwar & Badrinath

ॐ

Karpoor Gauram Karuna Avtaram
Sansaar Saaram Bhujgendra Haaram
Sadaa Vasantam Hridyaarvrinde
Bhavam Bhavaani Sahitam Namaami

—*Shiva Vandana*

Hail to Bhavani and to Lord Shiva
Whose complexion is the colour of camphor,
Who is compassion incarnate,
The in-dwelling essence of the world
Garlanded by snakes,
He dwells forever in the hearts of his devotees

I have visited the ancient town of Bageshwar in Kumaon in different times and moods: in thoughtless transition, in acceptance of yet another town of Kumaon, and in purposeful search. My most vivid memories are of the *samshan ghat* beside the river, of the temple of Baghnath and the unerring awareness that *samskaras* will surface and will pass in transition, if we remain detached.

Bageshwar

This ancient town is at the *sangam* or confluence of the Saryu and Gomati rivers. Baghnath Mahadeva's *mandir* was built by the Katyur *rajas* and later extended by the Chand *rajas*. The *lingam* here is believed to be *swayambhu* or self-emerging. Because Bhagwan Shankar is supposed to have given *darshan* as a *bagh*, the town received its name.

Near Bageshwar, Hairakhandi Babaji is known to have

frequented several places. He was often sighted at the *sangam* of Saryu and Gomati near Bageshwar and it is also said that he stayed at caves in this region. Babaji is also believed to have stayed at the ancient Baghnath temple. He was commonly known to live in *gufas* and Shiva temples and was seen walking alongside rivers. He was associated with Gorakhnath and *Panchnama Deva dhunas* in the Uttarakhand Himalayas, which were frequented by him. Whenever he was staying somewhere, the villagers would inevitably gather for his *darshan*, and consequently he would sometimes also stay in the villages.

Bageshwar is one of the ancient towns of Kumaon with a rich cultural and spiritual history. The *Uttarayani mela* is celebrated annually and it is said that Babaji was often in the vicinity at the time of the *mela* when many had the opportunity of receiving his *darshan*. Bageshwar has an old *sanyas* Datta (or Juna) *akhada*, familiar to most *sanyasins*. The Juna *akhada* is the oldest and largest *akhada* and Bhagwan Dattatreya is worshipped as the deity. The *mahant* of the *akhada* would welcome Babaji's arrival here with great eagerness. Many *tapaswi yogis* have been *mahants* here, like Mahant Ganga Giri-ji and Mahant Kishen Giri-ji.

Babaji was seen and known to have been accompanied by *sadhus* of all faiths and denominations. His disciples and devotees are cross-cultural, multi-religious, from all social backgrounds. They have nothing necessarily in common, other than their deep devotion and their sincere search for Truth.

Professor Kedar Dutt Joshi of Benares Hindu University had once spoken about his *darshan* of Hairakhandi Babaji at the age of nine in his village, Junail, 15 miles from Bageshwar. There is a Nanda Devi *mandir* at Junail where Hairakhandi Babaji spent a few days. On the way, he stopped at Joshi's house along with other *mahatmas*. Joshi-ji described him as '*tejaswi bal-surya rup*', energised like the rising sun. He said, living in Kashi, he had met thousands of *mahatmas*, but none like Hairakhandi Babaji. He added that Babaji could take *agni samadhi*, and that itself is the proof of his immortality. Kedar Dutt's *chacha* or father's younger brother, Baghambari Baba, was a disciple of Hairakhandi Babaji. He lived at Padampuri during Sombari Babaji's time.

Hairakhandi Babaji would, on occasion, go from Bageshwar onto Garur-Baijnath where there is an ancient Badrinath *mandir* where he would stay. Otherwise he would stay at the Baijnath temple now recognised as a heritage site. Here there is a remarkably beautiful ancient *murti* of Parvati Mata. There is a Kali temple close by, near where there is the *sangam* of the smaller tributaries of the Gomati from Kausani, and from Gwaldam and Badhaan Garhi. In Kumaon, these rivers are called Garh. The chief places near here are Chakrabarteshwar, Divyeshwar and Shakteshwar, all places of sacred energy. Between Bageshwar and Baijnath, there is an ancient fort with a Devi *mandir* that Babaji would visit.

Babaji would habitually take one of three directions. Sometimes from Bageshwar he would take the route to Almora through Kausani. From Kausani, he would also visit Pingnath Mutt in the village of Pingnath, the *mandir* in the dense forests beyond, and Budha Pingnath at 10,000 feet on the peak above, which was one of his *tapasya sthals.* He would also frequent Chedu village where he had a *kutia.* He would often stay at Bhatkoth, also known as Siddha Koth. Bhatkoth as well as Budha Pingnath and Pandukholi are known for their association with the *Pandavas and* are all *siddha sthans.* The Pandukholi *gufa* or cave is also referred to as Babaji's *gufa.* Many known and unkown *siddhas, rishis* and *yogis* through untold ages have done *tapasya* here.

From here, he would go on to Dunagiri or Dronagiri and Dwarahat. The Yogada Satsanga have since built an *ashram,* in memory of Lahiri Mahashaya's famed *darshan* of the immortal *yogi.*

Teerth Yatras to Badrinath

Hairakhandi Babaji is known to have visited Badrinath from

Bageshwar. On his way down from some of the higher Himalayan regions in the Nanda Khat area, he would proceed to Bageshwar and Baijnath along the river before travelling through Badhan Garhi, which has a Devi *shaktipeeth* at the boundary of Kumaon and Garhwal, where battles of yore had been fought. Along the banks of the river Pindar via Kulsari, Tharali, Naryan Bagarh. Simli, he reached Karanprayag, the *sangam* or confluence of the rivers Pindar and Alakananda.

Babaji had also been to Badrinath from *Siddhashram*, Sitlakeht via Ranikhet onto Dwarahat, Dunagiri and Gairsain, and further on through Adi Badri. From here, he is also said to have visited Naini Noti on the peak above. From Adi Badri, one of the *Panch Badris*, he was known to have gone to Badrinath via Karanprayag.

From Karanprayag the route leads to Nand Prayag. It is said that he would bathe in the river here and give *darshan* to *teerth yatris* or pilgrims, often having spontaneous *satsangha* during his *bhraman* or travels.

Badrinath, foremost among the *teerth sthans*, is Lord Vishnu's abode of meditation on the banks of the river Alakananda. Within the mighty Himalayas, *Nara-Narayana* stand here in silent contemplation, and *Neelkantha* remains in solitary splendour. *Tapaswi yogis* continue to perform austerities here. Pilgrims pay obeisance in this remote, desolate and spectacularly beautiful part of the Himalayas which leads further to the stark and largely inaccessible areas of the Himalayas, known almost only to adepts.

A myriad tales fan the imagination. Some of those who seek *darshan* here are compelled to do so by the bells of Badrinath. The *gufas* of Maharishi Bhrigu, Maharishi Veda Vyasa, Sri Ganesh and innumerable others, have the power to draw one to them. The icy winds that chill the body and numb the mind were the same winds that the *Panch Pandavas* had known on their way to *swargaloka*, when they departed this world. Lord Vishnu in the form of *Nara Narayana* is the eternal witness here. Lord Shiva, in his aspect as *Neelkantha*, protects his devotees. The *rishis, siddhas* and *yogis* have remained here in *samadhi,* both in physical and *sukhsham* or subtle form.

On my first visit here, I undertook the journey seemingly beyond my volition, in a surrendered flow of consciousness. I travelled here alone and sought the blessings of *Neelkantha* and of *Nara Narayana,* simply by being humbled in their presence to bow before them in awe and reverence. In my heart, was a prayer for protection and guidance to walk the razor's edge, discrimination to remain absorbed in the Self while completing *karmas,* and the *shakti* to do what must be done. I had heard this was a *tapasya sthal* of Sri Babaji, the immortal *yogi.* I had sought his *darshan* for understanding, knowledge and wisdom.

A few years later, inevitably, I returned to Badrinath. Accompanying Sri Gorakh Babaji and several other *yogis* to the *griha garbha* or sanctum sanctorum of the Badrinath temple, I bowed in humility and gratitude that my prayers had been answered manifold.

Chapter 14

Kali Kumaon

ॐ

Shraddha Van Labhte Gyanam

—Bhagwad Gita 4.38

One with faith attains Supreme Knowledge

The river Kali flows through the regions of Champavat and Lohaghat, where Haat Kalika is the *shaktipeeth*. This area in interior Kumaon has always been known as Kali Kumaon. The sacred places here have remained undisturbed, for the most part.

Rikheshwar

At one time, in the midst of dense forests, Rikheshwar is now accessible by road. On the banks of the confluence of two rivers, Rishi Ganga and Lohavati, this sacred place in the name of *rishis* is set amidst *devadar* trees. The Shiva temple here has an ancient *lingam*. Near the town of Lohaghat, a road from here goes to Mayavati. Babaji would go via Ghat to Rameshwaram, and onto Pithoragarh by the *paidal marg* or trail. Sometimes he would go from Rameshwaram to Chahaj where there is a *Pandava mandir* at which he stayed. From here, via the village of Jakhani, he would go to Gangolihat and onto Haat Kalika where Jangam Baba, a disciple of Hairakhandi Babaji had an *ashram*. Here, with Babaji's blessings, Jangam Baba opened a Sanskrit *vidyalaya* or school in the old tradition.

In this area, Hairakhandi Babaji is remembered well in

the villages of Pokhri, Barsayat, Chidgal, Dhyotung in the region of Gangolihat. From here, he would visit Dhaulinag and Berinag, where there are *nag mandirs*. It must be kept in mind that Babaji's *bhraman* was on foot through the Himalayas.

At the time of the *Mahabharat*, Lord Krishna defeated Kali Nag, who had made the waters of the Yamuna black. Lord Krishna thereafter graced the *nags* to reside in Uttarakhand. Dhaulinag, Berinag, Kalinag are some of the places associated with this legend, and each of the places has a Shiva *mandir*. In the *Treta Yuga*, Lakshman, brother of Sri Rama is believed to be a manifestation of Sheshnag, the *nag* or hooded serpent that protects Lord Vishnu. In a later epoch, during the *Dwapar Yuga*, Baldeva, Lord Krishna's elder brother is also regarded as a manifestation of Sheshnag.

From Berinag, the close view of the Himalayan peaks is spectacular. From here, a road leads to Koteshwar, Kala Muni, Munsiyari and onto Adi Kailash in Pithoragarh and Manasarovar-Kailash in Tibet. From Berinag, the road also leads to Patal Bhuvaneshwar.

I had first visited this region a couple of decades ago. More recently, during my current *bhraman* of the past three years, I have re-visited these areas.

Haat Kalika

The *mandir* at Gangolihaat is an ancient *shaktipeeth* regarded as an *up-peeth* or subsidiary of the *shaktipeeth* of Ma Kali at Kolkata. As at other *haats*, a regular marketplace would come up at regular intervals, visited by villagers from far and near. There are many stories told about the energy and power of worship at the *mandir* here. It is said that during the First World War, a ship was sinking in the high seas and the captain told everyone aboard to pray. A Kumaoni on board prayed to Haat Kalika, and it is said that many saw a hand appear from within the sea and push the ship towards shore. For many years, donations would come in from England and elsewhere in remembrance of this.

In olden times human sacrifice was conducted here, as it was at Devi Dhura in this region. It is believed to have been stopped by Adi Shankaracharya-ji, who evoked the *shakti* or energy of Kali to stop this practice. Hairakhandi Babaji was known to have spent time here. From here, through Berinag, Babaji would go via Khameri Devi to Shiakoth, Sangarh, Nakuri Patti and Shikhar Narayana onto Kapkot and then Bageshwar.

The temple here is an integral part of the Himalayan vista. Himalayan temples blend into the natural scenery, until and unless the onslaught of modernism and tourism overpowers their physical form.

Pokhri

The ancestral hometown of Durga Devi, wife of Dr. Hemchand Joshi, is Pokhri. Dr. Joshi recorded many incidents associated with Babaji's life in "*Mere Pyare Bhagwan Hairakhandi*". (My Beloved Lord Hairakhandi). Durga Devi's father, Ghananand Joshi and his wife were both devotees of Babaji. In 1911, the young Ghananand Joshi became very ill, and subsequently died. He was placed in the courtyard according to custom, before being taken for the final rites. His mother, a faithful devotee of Babaji said the body could not be cremated till the arrival of Babaji, and accordingly she sat in prayer to invoke Babaji, who soon arrived. She lamented the loss of her young son and the consequent state of his new bride. Babaji took a *daalim* or pomegranante branch from a tree and performed ritualistic awakening of the body. Thereafter, he said that milk from a lactating mother should be brought, which he poured into the dead boy's throat, and a gurgling sound emanated. Through *Mrit Sanjivani Vidya*, he brought the lad to life gradually. He said the youth should be taken indoors. Slowly warmth returned to his body and he began to breathe normally.

In this region, Khameri Devi is an old *shaktipeeth* in the forests, remote and highly energised. Khameri is one of Durga Mata's many names. Durga, Kali, Parvati, Uma, Gauri are some of the names by which the *Shakti* of Lord Shiva, his eternal consort, is addressed.

At Prachaar, above Sangarh, there is a *naun ling mandir.* Above is Shikhar Narayana, also called Shikhar Bhanaar or Mul Narayana, the *devata* or deity worshipped by the local population. There is a cave where Hairakhandi Babaji had done *tapasya* and also a *naula* or source of water. Other *yogis,* like Nantin Baba have also done *tapsya* here. Earlier, *yogis* always spent time in *tapasya* in caves and lived in *kutias* or humble dwelling places. They gave more importance to *tapasya* and *anushthan* or austerity and worship. Currently, the trend is towards preaching, building *ashrams* and organisations and having individual cult followings. The great *yogis* of old and those *yogis* who continue the eternal tradition, work silently for humanity. They live primarily in *ekant* or solitude, maintain *tapasya* and meet people spontaneously in the course of their daily lives.

Kapkot is beside the river Saryu which goes onto Bageshwar. These are all places of high energy, where *yogis* have lived or visited during their *bhraman kaal* or period of wandering. From Kapkot, Babaji would go to Bageshwar or to Sumgarh above Song, where there is a hot spring which is said to have emerged with Hairakhandi Babaji's *tapasya* and *anusthan.* There is a *mandir* and *gufa* here, and Babaji also had a *kutia* here. From Song, Babaji would proceed to Pindari glacier and the Nanda Khat region. Sumgarh on the hilltop was named in memory of Devi defeating the two *daityas,* Sumbh and Nishumbh, and thereafter resting here.

Like the mostly inaccessible areas around Badrinath and Gaumukh, the areas around Nanda Khat and Pindari have been the *tapasya sthal* of many Himalayan *yogis.* While trekkers and pilgrims regularly go along particular trails, there are many *gufas* and *tapasya sthals* in these regions which remain largely hidden. My own experiences at these sacred places have been of other dimensions, of deep awareness of the *kripa* of *rishis-munis* and *siddhas*, and an overwhelming humility in the realisation that it was destined.

Patal Bhuvaneshwar

Almost two decades ago, my husband Rajiv, our seven year old son Siddhartha, and I, were returning from a trek to Pindari glacier. At the village of Khati, we had spent the evening with Sri Gorakh Babaji, who was at the time travelling with several *yogis*. Hearing about Patal Bhuvaneshwar, we visited this sacred *mahagufa*.

My first visit to the sacred cave was when it was still barely known to the world, visited by *yogis* and occasional worshippers from Kumaon who were by tradition and faith exposed to the deeper significance of sacred *siddha sthans*. Entering here caused a significant shift in perspective. A cave of unimaginable form and proportions, it opened the doors to a spiritual world within physical co-ordinates. I realised the manifestation of divine energies and understood that many dimensions of living exist simultaneously. I glimpsed a world at once familiar and seemingly unknown or forgotten, to which I would return.

Patal Bhuvaneshwar is an ancient *mahagufa* close to Berinag and Gangolihat. Many *rishi-munis* have done *tapasya* here. Within, it is like an underground palace of yore. *Anusthan* would have been performed here for ages. The spiritual energies here speak of *siddhas, nags, yaksha, kinner, vidya-dhar* and *divya-manav*. When it was in the dense forests, it was a place of *gupt sadhana* for *siddha sadhaks* and *yogis*. It is considered likely that in the age of *gufas*, when kingdoms were ruled largely from *gufas*, it would have been a place of *siddha raj*. It is sometimes referred to as the *gufaon ki rani* or queen of *gufas*. The *gufa* is the mother of civilisation. Patal Bhuvaneshwar is believed to be limitless. It is said that there are *yogic margs* for *siddhas* which lead to Haridwar, Prayag, Kailash. As one cannot 'see' the flight path of airplanes, so also *yogic margs* are subtle pathways known only to *yogis*.

This *gufa* is believed to have been used by the *Pandavas*.

The *Pandava mandir* at Chahaj beyond Berinag is a reminder that these areas were frequented by the *Pandavas*. Guru Gorakhnath, Adi Shankaracharya, Maharishi Hairakhandi Babaji, who is regarded as Ashwasthama in these regions, are all believed to have come here. Many known and unknown *siddha yogis* are believed to have done sadhana here. There are *dhunas* of Guru Gorakhnath all over Uttarakhand. Shanakaracharya-ji is recorded as having visited Haat Kalika, where Devi gave him *darshan* as Jwala-ji. All three of them are *yatis, siddha yogis, rishis*. Both Shankaracharya-ji and Gorakhnath-ji are acknowledged as the manifestation of Bhagwan Shankar, belonging to the *Avatar koti* or manifesting divinity of Lord Shiva. It is believed that both of them, and also Hairakhandi Babaji had invoked the *Shakti* here, and diluted it, so that *Tantric* energy would not be misused in the *Kali Yuga*.

Rameshwaram

An ancient place, it is a symbol of the traditions of Bharat and regarded as a subsidiary of the *jyotirlingam* at Rameshwaram in Tamil Nadu. There is a *sangam* of Saryu-Sharda, and Panaar-Padmavati. During *Uttarayani* there is a *mela* here. There is a Shiva *mandir* as well as other *mandirs*. The *rajas* of Kumaon have performed *anushthan* and *yagya* here, and it has been the *tapasya sthal* of many *siddha yogis*. It is believed that Sri Gorakhnath had done *tapasya* here and the Nath *parampara* manintains the *dhuna* here and also performs worship at the Shiva *mandir* here. Being a place of spiritual energy, as well as having scenic splendour, it is ideal for *sadhana*.

Roads leading to different directions connect here. One road leads to Pithoragarh, Munsiyari and Dharchula, which was on the walking trail earlier. The second road through Chahaj, goes from Gangolihat to Berinag and leads to Bageshwar. From here one can go to Pindari glacier, as well as to Jageshwar and Almora. This was on the old walking trail. A third leads to Ghat, Lohaghat and Champavat onto Tanakpur, the rail head. The fourth road to Rangaur, Bhanoli, Saalam leads to both Devi Dhura and the Almora-Nainital side.

Hairakhandi Babaji had stayed at Rameshwaram and it continued to be one of his chief places of visit. From here he could go in different directions by the *paidal marg* or walking trail, which is all that existed at the time. He was a proponent of the philosophy that good thoughts should go in all directions and come in from all directions. The meeting of four pathways, like the *swastika*, is symbolic of this. During particular festivals, Hairakhandi Babaji had been known to take a sacred dip here and also give *darshan* to pilgrims. The local deities continue to be brought here for *snan* or ritual bath.

As at Kashi and Haridwar, it is believed that this is an auspicious place to leave the body or perform last rites. There is a *mahasamshan* or cremation ground here with a *chetan* or awakened Bhairav, which makes the place particularly significant from several perspectives.

It is also associated with Gorril Deva, with *dhunas* of Gorril Deva and Gorakhnath. It was here that Gorril Deva took his wooden horse to drink water. He was subsequently acknowledged as the rightful heir to the throne.

Gorakhnath, Talla Manch, Trijugi Narayan Dhuni

The *akhand dhuna* or eternal flame here, is believed to be continual through three *yugas* – *Treta, Dwapar* and *Kali Yuga.* On the main road from Champavat to Manch, the *dhuna* is at Talla Desh of Kali Kumaon. It is in the thick forest, close to Kali-Sarda, beyond which, visible to the eye, is Nepal. The water here is from a *kund* or *naula* or underground source. Gorakhnath and Matsyendranath are believed to have done *tapasya* here. Consequently many *yogis, sanyasins* and *sant mahatmas* have also done *sadhana* here. Manmunindra Hairakhandeshwar Acharya had done prolonged *dhuni tapasya* here at different times. The area of spiritual energy around the *dhuna* is known to be about five kms in circumference.

Pashupatinath *dhuna* at the edge of Bagmati in Nepal where Gorakhnath is the patron saint, Gorakhpur's Gorakhnath *dhuna* and this *dhuna* are spiritually connected. According to ancient tradition, the *bhog* and *puja* is supposed to be performed simultaneously at all three.

Much has been lost over time. One of the features of the *Kali Yuga* is that *tapasya* is at its lowest ebb. It is becoming increasingly difficult for *tapaswi yogis* to maintain the strict austerities that are fundamental to maintain spiritual energy. *Yogis* and *sants* need to return to these places and follow the ancient practices to maintain the living spiritual traditions that have enriched Bharat, the land of the Truth seeker. It is imperative that the sanctity of these sacred places remain undisturbed and protected so that *sant mahatmas* can continue to practice *sadhana* in solitude to maintain the *sanyas* traditions in their erstwhile purity.

CHAPTER 15

Saalam

ॐ

Siddhon ke marg sadhak ne paya

– *Sadhu Bani (oral tradition of sadhus)*

The path of the siddhas is revealed to sadhaks

On several earlier journeys, I had visited Saalam in Almora district, staying at different places during *bhraman* or wandering, until I had attained a deep familiarity with the people, the culture, the festivities, the traditions. Having lived in the area and having returned to spend much of my life in the Himalayas, particularly Kumaon, I know it well.

Saalam, known as Saalmali Parvat in the *Puranas* has many places of pilgrimage, *tapasya-sthals* and sacred rivers and rivulets. Pauneshwar, Basodhara, Airi Deva, Nag Deva, Hima Devi, Tankeshwar Mahadeva, Dhaam Deva, Dhurka Devi, Guna Ditya, Surya Mandir, Dhaula Devi, Koteshwar also known as Kotar or Jijulikoth, Airi Dhara at Rakshighat or Raksheshwar and Siddha Beri Chula, are some of the places of pilgrimage in this area.

One of the sacred rivers here is Padmavati, locally known as Panaar, which starts at Nag Deva. It is said that gold was mined from the sands here. Many smaller rivulets join it before it enters the Saryu-Sarda river at Rameshwaram beyond Ghat in Pithoragarh. Airi Ganga, also known as Ghatgaar, begins at Airi Deva. At Koteshwar, the Kheer Ganga or Devi Ganga with its source at Devi Dhura, joins it. Siddha Beri Chula is the source of the river Siddha Ganga, which joins at Airi Dhara. Thereafter, this joins the Padmavati.

Hairakhandi Babaji had done *tapasya* at all these sacred places, and had moved from village to village in this region, where old-timers still speak of him with unreserved devotion.

Airi Deva Barsigaja, Saalam, Almora

25 kms from Paharpani, and some 20 kms from Devi Dhura, Airi Deva is a place *of siddha* worship. Airi Deva is regarded as Arjun's *avatar,* and a knowledge-holder of the ancient *dhanur-vidya.* Set atop a hill amidst deodar trees, around the ancient *shaktipeeth* here, a *mandir* dominates the courtyard. There are a few *kutias* where *yogis* have lived and done *tapasya.* A large old *jheula* provides a great swing past trees, merging sky and earth. Out of character, the *jheula* is still not out of place. In another area of the hill, called Siddhamati, a Shiva *mandir* and Devi *mandir* have recently been built.

Great masters like Guru Gorakhnath are accepted as having graced this *siddha tapasya sthal.* A sacred *trishul* is worshipped at Airi Deva, through the performance of specific rituals. It is believed that it is a divine weapon in which the *shakti* or power of Brahma, Vishnu and Mahesh exists. Called *Airi Deva Raja Barsigaja,* or the shower of rain that descends spontaneously from the heavens, this *swayambhu trishul* is believed to have been established by *rishis.* Near the forest of Chira Tinmina Boxar, a village near Airikot, along with a *shankha* or conch shell, *ghanta* or bell, a *khadga* or sword and a *diya* or lamp, this was discovered.

These are worshipped at the *mandir* during times like *Navaratri.* At other times these are kept where they have been installed at a *mandir* in Kutoli, a village 3 kms away. Regarded as a *shaktipeeth* or an *up-peeth* of Manasarovar Kailash, the olden traditions are kept alive here through regular *anushthan* or ritual performance during *Navaratri* twice a year, and during the 22 days *jaagar* every three years, when the entire *Mahabharat* is recited in worship in the regional poetic language. The *pujaris* maintain *tapasya* when they perform *puja.* Maharshi Gorakh Babaji regularly participates in *anushthan* at this *tapasya sthal* of his.

According to local folklore about a century or more ago, when the *pujari* or priest was taking the *trishul* to the *mandir*, where it is brought for specific performance of worship, some *Naga sanyasins* challenged the *pujari* carrying it, saying that a *trishul* is Lord Shiva's weapon and the righteous owners are *Shaivite Naga sadhus.* It must be mentioned here that a *trishul* is not to be lightly associated - the rules and conduct of ownership is sacrosanct, as are the elements of worship related to it.

The *pujari,* who was at the time in austere ritual worship associated with the Barsigaja, stood the *trishul* on the ground saying he was not authorised to hand it to anyone, but if indeed it belonged to them, they could take it from where it stood. As a *Naga* reached towards it, it is said that the *trishul* of shining light sunk deeper into the ground and he was flung backwards. Accepting the divine nature of the weapon, and offering salutations, the *Nagas* left. At different *siddha peeths,* there are other divine *trishuls* like this.

Garg Chula

Close to Devi Dhura, this is also a *tapasya sthal* of Airi Deva, located at Chalsi. The *dhanush-baan* or bow and arrow at the temple here is particularly special, weighing 40 kgs. During the *anushthan* or ritual performance when the *siddhas* are invoked, the accepted *lakshan* or sign of the presence of a *siddha* is when a particular *tapaswi* easily picks up the *dhanush-baan* and strings it, to denote the presence of the *shakti,* before it subsides again. Here there is also a *murti* of Narayana. This is Maharishi Garg's *tapasya sthal,* and many *yogis* and *rishis* have done *tapasya* here, including Hairakhandi Babaji and Sombari Babaji.

Gorakhnath Dhuna, Granao, Saalam

Lord Shiva along with Guru Gorakhnath is worshipped at this ancient *mandir* in Granao or Guru-Gaon, at the edge of the village. This is also a *Panchname devasthan* and there is a small Purna Devi temple where the Devi is *chetan* or awakened and active. The tradition of *tapasya* at this 1,000 year old small and inconspicuous temple, is still strictly maintained. Many *tapaswis* have done *tapasya* here. Nearby, located on the ridge of a hill, set aside from the village settlement, amidst tall grass and swaying crops is a Gorril Deva *dhuna* and Airi Deva *mandir.*

Villagers always maintain the extreme sanctity of *siddha dhunas,* and keep a strict distance from them. Because of the inconspicuous nature of these *tapasya sthals,* they escape the attention of pilgrims and curious onlookers. Located where they are, no-one happens to wander into these places. For anyone tempted to seek out these places, caution is well advised, along with abiding respect for the ancient tradition whereby only he who maintains *tapasya* is allowed near these *dhunas.* Entry into the *griha garbha* or sanctum sanctorum of a *mandir* should not be attempted without checking from the local *pujari* who will be aware of the rules pertaining to the place of worship.

It is accepted that at *siddha dhunas,* Gorakhnath and the Nine *Naths* and 84 *Siddhas* can be invoked through intense *tapasya.* While these are sacred secret practices, and the *sadhana, tapasya* and any related incidents are not made public, all matters of the *siddha patal* are maintained in supreme sanctity. In a world grown increasingly faithless, it may be heartening to be reminded that nothing written in the Scriptures and ancient sacred texts is without reason or without truth. Moreover, eternal knowledge is never lost, neither born nor created, not subject to death nor destruction.

Debaal or Pauneshwar Mahadeva, Pughao

The Shiva temple of Debaal or Devalaya is at Pughau Barhakhot in Saalam, Almora. There was a Shiva *lingam* at which a cow would go daily and spontaneously bathe it with milk. There are ancient idols of Shiva-Parvati and Ganesh-ji. An idol of Surya Narayana has been stolen from here. The temple is in the style of Jageshwar. It is also known as Pauneshwar Mahadeva. On *Mahashivaratri* there is a *mela* here. People come to appease the powers that be, for rains as well as for the blessing of a child. Hairakhandi Maharaj along with Sombari Babaji and others had performed *yagya* here. Brahmachari Baba, Hari Chetanananda and Pitambari Baba have done *tapasya* here. Swami Trilochananda Giri, who had received *darshan* of Hairakhandi Babaji in his childhood and whose *samadhi* and *ashram* is at Paharpani, had done *tapasya* here.

Sri Hairakhandi Babaji had been known to visit Gorakhnath Dhuna, Granao and Pauneshwar. He would also visit Dungri village where his devotee, Pandit Manorath Pandey, father of Bhagirath Pandey, lived. This devotee is also mentioned in the hand-written manuscript of Siromani Pathak with relation to *Siddhashram.*

Swami Bhajan Giri known as Shastri Baba, born in an aristocratic family, was a scholar from Benares and did considerable work on astrology. He took *sanyas* in the late 1940's. He stayed here, as well as at Granao, among other places in Kumaon. A well-revered saint of the time, along with eight or ten other saints he did much work to keep the flame of spirituality alive.

Basodhara, Panaar

In a clearing beside the river Padmavati, is the temple dedicated to Chitreshwar Mahadeva. Hairakhandi Babaji along with many other *tapaswi yogis* have done *tapasya* here. The waters of Basodhara, or a thousand sources is considered sacred and is a place of pilgrimage. Near here is the Bhima Devi temple, where the Devi is a *shila* or natural stone, and not ascribed with form. Over time, the river here has lost much of its original glory.

In more recent times, Sri Ganga Giri also called Vikas Baba, lived at Basodhara as well as at Pauneshwar, Airi Deva and elsewhere in Kumaon. His *samadhi* is at Daulatpur, close to

Kathgodam, where the Inter-college was opened at his behest.

Nag Deva (Deo)

Below the road, reminiscent of Jageshwar, amidst a forest of *devadars* blessed by the gods, is a sacred place of antiquity. At the *sangam* or confluence of the rivers, Nag Ganga and Deva Ganga, there is a *dhara* or source of water, called Vishnu Kund which is regarded as particularly auspicious. It is beneath the temple dedicated to Lord Vishnu which was established to mark the *swayambhu* or self-emerging *shakti* in the form of a *shila* or sacred stone. Behind the Vishnu *mandir* is an old *devadar* tree. Legend says that there was a *Nag Yagya* held here by Maharaja Janmejaya, descendant of *Pandava* Maharaja Yudhisthir. It is said that all the *nags* or serpents offered themselves into the sacred fire. Takshat Nag is said to have taken the protection of Lord Indra, ruler of the celestial regions. At the time, influenced by Takshat Nag, Lord Indra himself was going to the *yagya,* which induced Lord Vishnu to manifest in blessing. To prevent an over-abundance of serpents, it was decided that when a serpent gives birth to innumerable serpents, it will devour its own. The few that will escape will maintain the ecological balance by which the species can continue.

There is a temple with a Shiva *lingam* here. Kumaonis regard it as a pilgrimage of Badrinath and Kedarnath. On a nearby mountain top is the *samadhi* of some *sadhus.* Close by, beside a rivulet, is a *samshan ghat* where funeral pyres burn. *Samshan ghats* are auspicious places for *darshan* of Shiva-ji, because it is believed that he visits them to cross devotees to other shores. On *Amavasya* or the night of the new moon, Shiva-ji is regarded as being present in his aspect as *Mahakaal,* ever-present, eternal, beyond time and death.

It is practically impossible to describe *siddha sthans.* For the most part they are rugged, harsh, austere, isolated. They are ferociously guarded and do not allow easy access. *Sadhana* and *tapasya* alone can reveal their many dimensions. There is nothing obviously visible to mark their threshold, no stated guidelines, no direction finders nor milestones. You return from them with nothing to show: empty-handed, as you went. Yet immeasurably richer.

Nag Dhuni or Siddha Dhuni, between Mournaula and Sahar Phatak

On a mountain peak, this *dhuni* is a *siddha sthal,* considered a powerful place for intense *sadhana.* In the old days, this was on the pilgrim trail to Kailash Manasarovar used by *yogis.* Many *tapaswis* have spent time here in *sadhana.* It is said that Hairakhandi Babaji would frequent this region. *Siddhas* in astral form are believed to be ever-present here. Seekers of Truth spend time at all *siddha sthans* seeking blessings to progress on the path. In the tradition of *siddhas,* the formless, attribute-less nature of divinity itself is worshipped and the grosser levels must be transcended continuously, in order to be able to receive the teachings that are themselves expressed subtly and received wordlessly. Only one who is established with inner vision can tread this pathless path.

swadhyaya

Chapter 16

Lakes of Nainital District

ॐ

Yogash Citta Vritti Nirodhah

– *Yoga Sutras of Patanjali 1.2*

Yoga is perfect restraint of fluctuations of consciousness

While Nainital is primarily known as a tourist destination, the compelling attraction and tranquillity that visitors often experience here has much to do with its spiritual history as a *sadhana sthal.* The scenic lakeside town is also the district headquarter with a circumference that includes many places of *sadhana* and several Himalayan lakes.

Nainital

Nainital is an ancient *shaktipeeth* of Devi. Among the 108 *shaktipeeths,* it is associated with Sati's eye. During a landslide at Naina Peak, now referred to as China Peak, the ancient *mandir* which housed the natural *prateek* of Devi was destroyed. The Devi was taken to the current location and a temple was established here.

As at Nanda Devi *mandir* in Almora, the temple has idols of Maha Kali, Maha Saraswati and Maha Lakshmi. Ma Jagdamba, or cosmic creation, is worshipped in her triple aspect associated with Lord Shiva, Lord Brahma and Lord Vishnu, as the *shakti* in creation, preservation and dissolution. Close by is a Shiva *mandir.* Beside this is a *Naun Graha mandir,* dedicated to Surya and the planets. About fifty years ago, a Radha-Krishna *mandir* was also established. There is a new Santoshi Mata *mandir*. There is a *yagya-shala* here. Earlier, there was a 2 room *dharamshala* mainly for *sadhu-sants,* which is no longer there, and a hall for *satsangha* which has since been converted into a shopping area. *Nandashtami* is celebrated with Nanda and Sunanda being carried in ceremonial procession in a *doli* or palanquin.

Paashan Devi on Thandi Sarak is an ancient *gufa,* believed to be an *adi shakti.* There are several *gufas* where *sadhu-sants* had done *tapasya* in the old days. These *gufas* have become polluted now and are no longer used for *tapasya.* Older residents of Nainital, whose ancestors had known Hairakhandi Babaji claim that he would dive into the lake and reappear after several hours. He is believed to have mentioned that below the lake there are *jal gufas* where *siddha yogis* have remained *samadhisht* for many ages. There are many incidents relating to Hairakhandi Babaji at Nainital, including Commisioner Henry Ramsay's encounter of him near Pashan Devi. Also known is the incident when Babaji lit his *dhuna* on Mall Road at a time that Indians were not permitted to use that road.

Nainital is not an ancient town like Almora, whose cultural history dates far back. In earlier days it was a place of pilgrimage and of *tapasya.* Before 1839, it was a village. The popularity of Nainital grew after the British discovered it and chose to occupy it, building it as a summer retreat and thereafter, establishing it as a summer capital of the state of Uttar Pradesh. The religious and spiritual significance of the town has been over-shadowed because of its popularity as a scenic hill station.

There are other *sant-mahatmas* who lived in Nainital at a time when it was not primarly a tourist destination but was known as a *shaktipeeth.* Trilochananda Giri, who had been inspired to take *sanyas* after his childhood *darshan* of Babaji, had done *tapasya* at Nainital in *taat* or sackcloth in the 60's. Liladhar Bughani of Paharpani who worked in the DM's office, was given an additional 15 minutes time off for lunch, because he would take a meal for him daily. Sitaram Baba, who passed away a decade ago, did *sadhana* here and had made the Hanuman *mandir.* He is different from another great saint by the same name who currently lives in Bridh Jageshwar.

The Gufa Mahadeva at Nainital is a natural *gufa* located in Krishnapur, Tallital below GIC College. There are several streams which flow here. Many saints have done *sadhana* here. Both Swami Vivekananda and Sri Aurobindo have visited here. Hairakhandi Babaji is known to have stayed here. He and Sombari Babaji would visit together on their way up to Nainital by the walking trail which still exists and is a short-cut, compared to the longer metalled road. Until three decades ago, Sri Amar Giri resided here.

Khurpatal

On the Kala Doongi road, 3 miles from Nainital, Khurpatal was earlier reached on foot. There is a small lake and also a cave, called Narayani *gufa,* which is well above the lake. Hairakhandi Babaji would pass this way often and had stayed here several times. From here, Babaji would go to Sitabani, Kotabagh, where Mata Sita is supposed to have lived. The small *mandir* in the barely inhabited dense forests of Sitabani, in tiger country, is a poignant reminder of Mata Sita's life of *tapasya.* Even today, ascetics spend time in intense *sadhana* here.

At Khurpatal, Hairakhandi Babaji is still a household name among the older residents who speak of him with deep reverence. Babaji would usually stay at an old temple near Khurpatal, or sometimes at some devotee's home. Here too he is mostly referred to as Ashwasthama. The famed story of the young man who had sought him out hoping to ascertain whether he was indeed Ashwasthama, occurred here. When the man arrived, Babaji suggested a bath in the lake. Taking off the cap he habitually wore, he bathed in the river. The young man was in a state of trance and had forgotten his initial intention of seeing the crown of Babaji's head to verify if he was Ashwasthama. When he remembered it, Babaji answered his unspoken query, "Meet a saint or an evolved soul with respect. Only those blessed by God can recognize a saint. He who has a pure heart attains the grace of saints."

Sat Tal Bankhandi

Beyond the now popular lakeside resort of Bhimtal is Sat Tal, a deep lake within a forested region. In the jungles here is a place called Bankhandi, where it is believed that the *sapt rishis* have done *tapasya*. Many known and unknown saints have done *sadhana* here. Hairakhandi Babaji is said to have stayed here awhile.

Nantin Baba who had an excellent knowledge of Himalayan herbs, was a well-known saint who lived in the Sat Tal region till two decades ago. Originally from Madhya Pradesh, he left home as a young boy and was a *tapaswi yogi* whose *sanyas* name was Siddha Giri. He had stayed with one Sitaram Baba, different from both the saints mentioned earlier in context of Nainital and Bridh Jageshwar. He had travelled widely in the Narmada region, stayed at Ayodhya and spent some 25 years of his life in the Kumaon Himalayas, including three years or more in the Pindari region. His *ashram* at Haldwani is now maintained by his devoted disciple, Shankar Baba, whose knowledge of Himalayan herbs was gained from Nantin Baba.

Near Bhimtal, Nal-Damayanti Tal is associated with *Raja* Nal and his queen Damayanti. Near Bhimtal is Karkotak peak named after the serpent Karkotak, believed to be the *guru* of *nags*. The description of Nal, Damayanti and Karkotak is in the *Srimad Bhagavat Purana*. When *Raja* Nal had lost his kingdom in a game of *pasha*, and was compelled to roam these forests, he had left Damayanti in this region, determined to spare her a lifetime of misery in accompanying him.

Karkotak, cursed by Narad Muni, was unable to move. During a raging fire, he had requested Nal to rescue him. Nal had received a boon of protection against fire so that he would remain untouched by it. When Nal lifted him up, Karkotak requested him to walk ten steps with him before putting him down. On the way, Karkotak repeatedly put his fangs into him, and Nal's complexion changed colour. Karkotak explained that he was hurting *Kali Yuga* within Nal, which had clouded his judgement and led to his consequent misfortunes. He said this would also help him to conceal who he really was during his time of *tapasya.* Karkotak further blessed Nal with *divya vastra* and *divya swarup* or divinity, whenever required. Accordingly, he was able to prove who he was when he met Damayanti again. It is said that he who takes the name of Nal, Damayanti and Karkotak diminishes the impact of the *Kali Yuga* on his mind. When our mind is deluded, we suffer from ignorance, and our actions are a consequence of that. When our mind is attached to the Eternal Self, we are ever perfect and free.

Gethia

Having spent three summers and more at Gethia in Nainital district, the time here was of intense *swadhyaya.* How can lifetimes of experience be captured in a few words? It was a magical time. It was meant to be.

The lake at the side of the *ashram* would fill with the rains and dry out in the summer. It is said that the dark colour of the waters of the lake was from the bloody battle fought here several centuries ago. On the route to the higher Himalayas, many *sant-mahatmas* have been here, currently as well as in the past. The location of the *ashram* is at an old *sadhana sthan* and there has been a *kutia/ashram* here from the 13th century. The outward manifestation has changed from time to time.

Within the physical space, there is an immeasurable depth of living though many dimensions that many *sadhaks* have experienced here. As is common at places like this, there are several stories told about the energy of the place. Certainly a large spectrum of living was witnessed without filters.

My own experiences here have been a sense of immense familiarity and belonging. For me, it was a protected space where I was able to do prolonged *sadhana* and *swadhyaya*.

Visibly, my husband, Rajiv and I learnt, as well as taught, many techniques and practices of *Yoga*. We received contemporary and ancient teachings of the *yogi* traditions. There was a library of books we enjoyed. We experienced the lifestyle of *yogis* in an *ashram*. We interacted with the many seekers, devotees and others who came here. We were an integral part of the *ashram* during our stay. We woke to glorious days and slept in alert awareness.

Simultaneously, Sri Gorakh Babaji gave *darshan* of the *yogi, siddha* and *rishi* traditions, revealed through his *dhuna,* which he maintains in strict privacy in the ancient tradition. I re-connected with my eternal spiritual heritage. I recognised who I am and why I am here. It was the fulfilment of a promise that continues.

CHAPTER 17

Ranibag

ॐ

Asango Ahamanango Ahamalingo Ahamaabhangurah
Prashanto Ahamananto Ahamamalo Aham Chirantanah

-Adi Shankaracharya's Vivek Chudamani verse 489

I am unattached, without form, beyond birth and death, serene and infinite am I, perfect and eternal.

Ranibag is barely a couple of kms from Kathgodam at the foothills of the Kumaon hills. From Gethia, I had been here several times with Sri Gorakh Babaji. Staying at Kathgodam, reaching here on foot, this was without doubt my most memorable visit here.

We went to the old Shiva temple where Hairakhandi Babaji had been known to offer worship in the past. At one time, he was looking after a *sanyasin* who was ill and staying at Surya Devi, Gollapar, some 9 miles away in the hills. Hairakhandi Babaji would come from there to bathe in the river at Ranibag daily to be at the temple at 4 am.

The current *pujari*, Mahant Maheshananda Ban, who is a Goswami, or descendant of a *Dasnam sanyasin*, talks of the time his *nana* or maternal grandfather was the *pujari* of the temple. When he would come to offer worship at the temple he would find that *puja* had already been done within the locked temple. Surmising that someone had made a duplicate key, keen to catch the culprit, he decided to keep vigil through the night. In the moonlight he saw a tall, imposing *mahatma*, in a white *chola* or gown, head covered, walk down to the river. When he was mid-stream, the *pujari's* grand-father describes the sight, 'like an elephant splashing'. When describing Hairakhandi Babaji's gait, Siromani Pathak had also described it, 'like an elephant moving regally, he would walk through forest paths, able to reach anywhere'.

After bathing in the river the *mahatma* walked towards the temple. As he approached the gate, to the utter amazement of the *pujari,* the gate opened itself and the *mahatma* walked in. After he had done *puja* and walked out, the gate locked again. Speechless, the *pujari* did not have the courage to approach the *mahatma.* Thinking about it the entire day, he stayed up the next night again waiting for the *mahatma.* After Babaji bathed he waked towards the temple. The gate opened of its own accord as he approached. The *mahant* came out of his hiding place. Babaji laughed and said, "Since yesterday you have been tailing me. I am Hairakhan Baba. I am staying at Surya Devi."

Maheshananda Ban says, "of course he had all *vidyas,* he was Guru Dronacharya's son. Kripacharya-ji and Ashwasthama-ji are the two *chiranjeevis* who survived the *Mahabharat.* He has roamed the world so long. In his wanderings he has stayed at Hairakhan also. My *nana* said, when the villagers saw smoke coming from the *gufa* at Hairakhan, they went there and met him. My *nana* used to talk about him. He said he was very tall and had a clean unbearded face. He wore white clothes and a *kanchopi topa.* No-one could see the top of his head where the *mani* or jewel had been and be able to remember it."

Sitting under a tree beside the temple listening to him talk, I sipped the tea prepared by Swami Brahmananda Puri of the Niranjani Akhara. Before that, I had sat at Swami Brahmananda-ji's *dhuna* listening to the conversation between him and Sri Gorakh Babaji.

For many years, the quiet, gentle *sanyasin* would come to

Sri Gorakh Babaji

Sacred waters at Ranibag

Chitrashila at Ranibag

the *Chitrashila* at the banks of the river every morning to recite the *Shiva Sahasranam.* Maheshananda Ban suggested that Swami Brahmananda-ji stay there. Accordingly from '93, he has been living in his *kutia* beside the adjacent Shiva *mandir.* He says, "Here Shiva-ji does everything. This is my experience."

The *teerth* of Chitrashila is mentioned in the *Manas Khanda* of the *Skanda Purana,* where all the *teerth sthans* of Kumaon are described. In the *Satya Yuga* it was said to be created by *shilpi* Vishwakarma. The waters here are as sacred as at Haridwar. Despite the vast quantities of water that have flowed over this sacred rock, it has remained the same.

When *rishi* Markandey had done *tapasya* here, he was given *darshan* by three *devas.* It is said that Nara-Narayana later went to Badrinath, but Bhagwan Shankar remained here. Markandey asked Shiva-ji to show him his *maya,* to show him *pralaya kaal* or the time of cosmic dissolution. Markandey realised that there was nothing but *jal* or the waters and *akash* or ether. Markandey saw a banyan leaf floating, and on it, in *suksham* or subtle form, was Bal Mukund or the child Krishna. Markandey realised that there was none but him who witnessed and this child from whom creation began. After that, Bhagwan Shankar withdrew his *maya* and Markandey was blessed to become a *chiranjeevi.*

A steep 6 mile ascent from here leads to Markandey *kund* or Markandey *ashram,* where many *rishi-munis* have done *tapasya.*

The *sapt rishis* too are believed to have done *tapasya* here. In the *Satya Yuga, rishi* Satrupa is said to have done *tapasya* here for 36 years, after which he received *darshan* of Lord Shiva. Hairakhandi Babaji had done *tapasya* both at Chitrashila and at the nearby *gufa,* which is remembered chiefly in the name of Jiya *Rani.* Here, in the eleventh century, a devotee of Lord Shiva, *Rani* Jiya, regarded as a *siddha rani* or queeen, did *tapasya* at Chitrashila. The place is named after her – Ranibag. It is said, that as she bathed in the river, a long lock from her tresses, become golden by prolonged *tapasya* in the sunlight, tore off and flowed down the river. Seeing this, tantalised by her imagined beauty, a Muslim invader came in search of her. As he approached her, she ran towards the *gufa* or cave. It opened up to let her in but closed so she could not be followed. Two roads opened from within, one leading to Haridwar and the other in the direction of her gathered forces. Her nine lakh Katyuri forces are then believed to have overcome the invader. She herself is said to have become *antardhyani* or disappeared, having attained liberation.

My earlier visits had been during the day, and the intense vibrations of the place had always been somewhat masked by the business of living and dying that is apparent here, at the *samshan ghat* beside the river.

Now, the sun rising over the hill caused the cold waters of the night to sparkle and glow. It was a new dawn. The waters washed the ashes of yesterday. Walking over the stones, here and there the signs of loss and grief were apparent – hair shorn in *mundan* to perform the last rites, bangles broken in widowhood, remnants of torn lives. And the spirits of the dead who had been left for their first night alone, where the living cannot follow them. Death is the ultimate equaliser. In the face of it, nothing else remains. And Lord Shiva indeed walks between the great funeral pyres, to create again from *bhasma.*

Surya Devi

The *shaktipeeth,* Surya Devi is in the forested foothills of Kumaon Kailash. It is here that Babaji is known to have stayed when he was looking after an ailing *sadhu.* On other occasions too, he had been here.

Surya Devi can also be reached from the village of Hairakhan. Beside it, there is a small rivulet whose source is somewhere in the hills above Hairakhan. Some other rivulets also join it. There is no *mandir* here. There is a small *gufa* and some *shilas* or sacred stones. Many different *yogis* have done *tapasya* here. It is a *tapasya sthal,* particularly for those worshipping Devi or Kali. One trail from here also leads to Babaji's *kutia* at Ghumani Bhagat's home, about 6 miles from here.

Kali Chaur

Across the bridge from Kathgodam station along the Chaur Galia road, about 3 kms away, is the *shaktipeeth* Kali Chaur. From here, the road goes on towards Hairakhan through the forests. During the *Navaratri* twice a year locals come here on pilgrimage, as do devotees from elsewhere. The *mandir* has an awakened Devi, and worship is maintained here. The Devi is believed to protect the people, their homes and their livestock. Devotees come here to seek fulfilment for their wishes. It is a *sadhana sthan* for those worshipping Ma Kali. There are *dhunas* of *sadhus* here, and even today there is generally one or two *sadhaks* practicing austerities here. Hairakhandi Babaji would regularly visit all *teerthsthans* and *tapasyasthals* on his trails between his chief *tapasya sthals*.

Hairakhandi Babaji's kutia at Ghumani Bhagat's home, Deola

Maharishi Hairakhandi Babaji's famed *chimta* remains where Babaji had placed it 110 years ago at Ghuman Singh Naula's house in Chaur Galia Road, Deola village. Hairakhandi Babaji would visit his devotee known as Ghumani Bhagat, originally a resident of Naula village, Padampuri. Babaji's *chimta* and *kalash* still stand within the little *kutia*, his *dhuna* remains. The *kutia* remains almost untouched since his last visit here, though his devotee has long gone. Ghumani Bhagat's grandson, Kishen Singh stays with his family, in the adjacent *'pucca'* or cemented house beside the *kutia*. Their old home opposite the *kutia* is still intact though in disrepair.

Sri Gorakh Babaji, who had visited him a decade ago had instructed Kishen Singh not to pull down Babaji's *kutia* as intended. At that time, when Kishen Singh's mother was still alive, Sri Gorakh Babaji had purified the place and re-awakened the *dhuna*. He had also done *puja* and lit an *akhand diya*. Visiting here, he now pointed out the fact that their new home was too close to Hairakhandi Babaji's *kutia.* Ghumani Bhagat's grandson readily agreed. He said Babaji's *kutia* wall had fallen because of it, and he realised Babaji's displeasure. He had the wall repaired so it is much the same as it had always been. Sri Gorakh Babaji walked into the inner room where Hairakhandi Babaji had often stayed. He commented on the fact that worship is not being performed here anymore.

From outside the room, Kishen Singh's wife's voice could be heard. She complained that her husband was not regular about lighting the *diya* and when he missed for several days or on festivals, she dreamed of Hairakhandi Babaji, whom she had never met physically. She said that she saw him standing at the doorway of the *kutia* looking in, leaving without entering, seemingly saddened. She adds that because women are not allowed into that area she is unable to keep it clean or worship there, though she maintains the rest of the *kutia.*

Within the inside room, Sri Gorakh Babaji offered *bhog* and lit the *diya* where Babaji would sit in contemplation. As the *diya* sprang to life, a clearly visible *jyoti* extended along the *chimta* behind it. Ghumani Bhagat's grandson enquired from me, "What is it?"

I replied, "You can see it for yourself."

Sri Gorakh Babaji told Ghumani's grandson, "Clean up the place. If it be *Maharaj's* wish, I will come and stay here and perform *anushthan* sometime."

We walked through the fields to the main road and left to visit the neglected *samadhi* of Sri Ganga Giri, known as Vikas Baba, further down the road at Daulatpur. Thereafter, we visited a couple of other places also connected to the old tradition, before we boarded the old meter gauge train from Lal Kuan to Mathura, another reminder of a time fast fading away.

Chapter 18

Foothills of Kumaon

ॐ

Namah Shivabhyam Kalinashanabhyam
Kankala kalyana Vapurdharabhyam
Kailashasailasthitha Devatabhyam
Namoh Namah Shankara Parvatibhyam

– Adi Shankaracharya's Uma Maheshwara Stotram verse 7

Praise be to Shiva-Parvati who destroy the ignorance of this dark age,
Inherent in that which manifests, resplendent in all that is pure and good,
My salutations to thee whose abode is the eternal Kailash

In early winter, I was in the foothills of Kumaon. This time there were several others accompanying Sri Gorakh Babaji. The week spent at Haldwani was essentially a time of waiting for me. I was eager and impatient to proceed to the village of Hairakhan, and to pay my respects at Kumaon Kailash. It is one of the *up-peeths* or subsidiaries of Manasarovar Kailash in Tibet, eternal abodes of Lord Shiva.

Keenly aware that one cannot force *darshan* or speed it, aware that there are *karmic* cycles to be completed before one returns to that state of One-ness which allows one to perceive the infinitely subtle realms of *siddhalok,* I was struggling to overcome my physical self and the modifications of the mind.

At Haldwani, I sought the wheat among the chaff in my many interactions here. Sri Gorakh Babaji repeatedly reminded me that there are past *samskaras* which must sometimes surface and the *karmas* therein be completed. "All the oil has been emptied from the vessel, and yet some still sticks to the side of the vessel. That too must be washed away."

I waited for the day we would head for Hairakhan. I waited for *Kartik Purnima*. With Babaji were two of his devotees, whom he was at constant pains to purify through *karma yoga*. All the others who were accompanying Babaji, or who had sought to travel with him on this *yatra*, had already dropped out. I witnessed the *lila* that preceeded yet another sacred *yatra*. I was aware that it is Shiva-ji's *lila*, Mahadeva's *maya*, almost impossible to behold and maintain equanimity. It is not possible to attain Lord Shiva's grace by effort and determination alone. It is He Himself who bestows grace. And so I struggled for *kripa*.

Sri Gorakh Babaji stresses the importance of *nishkama karmayoga*, without which we cannot be purified. He always says, "This is a blessed age, so little do you have to do to receive blessings. In this age, the many faults of the mind are forgiven, because in the *Kali Yuga*, it is the mind that gets disturbed. Even great *gyanis* must perform *karmayoga* to remain in equanimity." He also stresses the importance of *japa*. "*Hari naam* will take you across the ocean of *samsara*."

He has said, in today's times, because of the possibility of misuse, most powers have been withdrawn. The Kalki *avatar* will come to restore the balance in keeping with the promise that Narayana himself returns to establish Truth in every age as the *nimitta avatar*. Saints and sages are a reminder of this Truth, the *nitya avatar* of Narayana, through whose medium the Truth manifests, through whom we are reminded of those Eternal Truths.

Spending a week at Haldwani, I visited many *ashrams, sadhu-sants, vidwans* and traditional Kumaoni homes with links to Hairakhandi Babaji. At this time, the veteran freedom fighter from Paharpani, Pandit Lokmani Sharma and his seven living sons, were hosting a week-long *Bhagawat.* Sri Gorakh Babaji would daily grace the *satsangha* there.

At Nantin Babaji's *ashram*, presided by his disciple Shankar Baba, the Lakshmi-Narayana *yagya* was being held. Shankar Baba had lived with Nantin Baba for a decade before Nantin Baba left his mortal body in the mid-80's.

One morning, before proceeding on the day's non-stop visits, Sri Gorakh Babaji left me here telling Shankar Baba to give me some tea. He replied, "I won't give her, or anyone else, tea. But I will give her milk."

Babaji suggested that he give me a quiet place to sit, adding, "don't let her run away till I return".

Shankar Baba asked, "does she do that too?" I shook my head in protest laughing at the image Babaji had portrayed. Shankar Baba assured Babaji, "Don't worry, we will tie her up if she tries to leave."

Shankar Baba gave me a glass of milk, while I sat in his crowded little room. Within five minutes, sensing my preference for solitude, he took me to a large hall, where I spent several hours alone in unbroken silence, except for the occasional visit from Shankar Baba who placed fruits, sweets and another glass of milk in front of me. Shankar Baba is a quiet, humorous, briskly active *sadhu,* who runs the *ashram* with efficiency maintaining age-old traditions. He offered solicitude and blessings to the constant stream of visitors who came.

In the evening *satsangha,* Sri Gorakh Babaji spoke of the wisdom of the *Gita.* He also spoke of the well-loved saint Nantin Baba. My only verbal exchange with Shankar Baba was when I left with Babaji, *"Har Har Mahadeva."*

Early morning walks every day were invariably with Pandit Jayadautt Kandpal, a learned Sanskrit scholar, well-versed in the *Puranas, Vyakarana, Karma Kand,* and the *Bhagawat.* On the outskirts of Haldwani, we walked beside planted fields and the occasional *gaushala* where cows are reared. Ahead, beckoning, was Kailash. Surya Narayana, in His visible aspect as the Sun nourishing us with life-giving energy, re-vitalised me and remained the silent witness.

One morning, we visited Pundarikaksha *Maharaj* at his *ashram.* I spent several hours listening while he reminisced. Born in 1926, in 1934-'35 when he was less than 10, he recalls his meeting with Hairakhandi Babaji. On his way back from school, near a stream beside a temple, he saw a *mahatma,* accompanied by someone else, sitting on a rock by the temple. The saint spoke to the young lad, "I have two kinds of *roti* (bread) – one is thick and smeared with *ghee* but it is *jootha* (has been tasted). The other is thin and dry. Which will you choose to eat?"

Pundarikaksha-ji explains that he was a young lad, driven by hunger and desire, natural for a boy of limited means. It was this, rather than any elevating thought, that prompted his reply, "I will have the *jootha roti.*" Pundarikaksha-ji says, "Witness the Lord's *lila.* Babaji pleased by my choice, gave me the *roti,* his blessings and some of the most important lessons of my life, which had a lifelong impact on me."

Some 15 days later, a little above this spot, he heard a group of people passing by. Hiding in the bush, he saw Hairakhandi Babaji with some 20 people. Babaji ushered them on, remaining alone behind. He looked around him and opened the white headscarf he wore. From above, the boy saw a *gaddha* or deep pit, the size of a large *amla,* on the crown of his head. Pundarikaksha-ji says again, "See the divine *lila. Maharaj* quickly covered his head and walked on."

Pundarikaksha-ji says, "Science cannot reach or explain those spiritual realms. Scientific reason can explain the *annamaya kosha, pranamaya, manomaya* and the *vigyanmaya kosha.* Beyond is the *anandamaya kosha,* known by *yogis,* wherein the *maya* itself becomes lost and only *ananda* remains –*ananda hi ananda* – the pure bliss of divinity. Who has known this bliss? *Yogis,* known and unknown."

Speaking of some of the great *tapasya sthals* of Kumaon, Pundarikaksha-ji particularly refers to Vashishtha *ashram* at Sukha Narayana, above the source of the Saryu, some 20 miles beyond Bageshwar. He mentioned that only a handful of *yogis* have been to this sacred *siddha sthal* at 9,000 feet, crossing impossibly difficult terrain. Among those who have been here within living memory are Nantin Babaji, Purnananda Giri-ji, Akhandananada Giri-ji, Pundarikaksha-ji and Gorakh Babaji.

Pundarikaksha-ji continued his talks about the many great sages and saints he had met in the Himalayas, always adding, "There are others too, unknown, both in the past, and now. Who knows the divine bliss they have known, except they themselves, because it is not possible to experience what another experiences, it is not possible to know the *ananda* of another."

He points out that the rational temperament will deny the experiences of the great Meera Bai. As a child when the saint who stayed in her parent's house was departing, the child Meera, was reluctant to see him go. To appease the child, she was asked, "What do you want as a parting gift?"

Meera chose the idol of Lord Krishna. The saint told her, "You must offer *bhog* daily. Only after that should you eat." For seven days, Meera offered food and it remained untouched.

With the innocence of childhood, she pleaded, "Why do you receive his offerings and not mine?" She remained hungry until the Lord himself was compelled to appear and partake of the *bhog*. As the milk was drunk, Meera, snatched it away, exclaiming, "For seven days I have remained hungry, and now you are finishing it all without leaving any for me."

CHAPTER 19

Hairakhandi Babaji's Ashram at Kathgaria

ॐ

Kastvam ko aham kuta ayatah
Ka me Janani ko meTatah,
Iti paribhavaya sarvam asaram
Vishvam tyaktva swapna vicharam

-Adi Shankaracharya's Bhaja Govindam verse 23

Who are you? Who am I? Wherefrom did I come? Who is my mother? And who my father? Contemplate this. Abandon all else that is nought but a mere dream

Haldwani, Kathgaria and Kathgodam are now almost part of the larger Haldwani area. Recently, habitation has increased upto Ranibag. At the time when Hairakhandi Babaji spent time in *tapasya* at Kathgaria, it was in the midst of jungles. Commisioner Henry Ramsay, who had become his devotee after several mystical encounters of him, allotted this land to Babaji.

Kathgaria was one of Hairakhandi Babaji's main *tapasya sthals.* He sat under a *haldu* tree, which thereafter, became intertwined with a *bat vriksha* or banyan tree and a *peepal* or variety of fig, also known as Bodhi tree because the Buddha had attained enlightenment under it. Seemingly from one tree, different branches and leaves exist. All three trees are regarded as sacred.

Govardhan Suyal, the old *pujari* who died at the turn of this century aged 104 years, used to speak with awe about Hairakhandi Babaji. An incident that he talked about was how Babaji had sat within a heap of *kanda* or dry cakes of dung used for burning, and asked for it to be lit. The young Govardhan thought it was the last he would see of Babaji. Sometime later, returning there, he found Babaji sitting on his *asana*.

At Kathgaria, Babaji established Kedareshwar, a Shiva *lingam* with the *shakti* of Kedarnath. At many of the places where he established a *mandir*, the *shakti* or spiritual energy invoked was of an existing Shiva *shaktipeeth*. He did this primarily so that those who could not undertake a long journey, could have *darshan* there itself. There is also a small Bhairav *mandir* near Kedareshwar.

At the entrance, a *sant kutir* with a *dhuna*, established by Hairakhandi Babaji, saw many great *sant-mahatmas* of the time visit and stay. Later, a Devi *mandir*, a Hanuman *mandir* and a Bhairav *mandir* have been constructed. Though there is a Trust to look after this sacred *tapasya sthal*, other than daily *puja* performed here by the family of *pujaris* who have been here since Hairakhandi Babaji's time, nothing has been done to maintain the place. An inter-college has since been opened in the *ashram* compound.

In the 50's, Mahendra Brahmachari-ji, did *tapasya* and visited several places associated with Hairakhandi Babaji to write various inspired accounts about him. At the time he had built a *mandir* here dedicated to Babaji, with an idol of him.

He also built a temple dedicated to him called Shyam Sadashiva Kunj at Vrindavan, where an idol of Hairakhandi Babaji was established. Over time, after Mahendra Brahmachari passed away, his devotees added his idol and have made this as much a *mandir* for him as for Hairakhandi Babaji.

Bhole Baba had expanded the temple at Vrindavan. His

devotees, in turn, have also added worship of him in living memory of Hairakhandi Babaji. In the *siddha* tradition, *siddhas* do not need to work directly, but can quite easily work through the medium of other *siddhas* or *siddha sadhaks.* When any work needs to be completed, a fully prepared *sadhak* or pupil can, with the grace of the *siddha* lineage, do the required work.

Because of the condition of disrepair at Kathgaria, and the fact that vagrants would sit under the sacred tree here with scant respect, and use the *sant-kutir* indiscriminately, Sri Gorakh Babaji stayed here awhile in *tapasya* to protect the place and the spiritual environment. He had a boundary erected around the sacred tree, and had the *sant kutir* repaired. It is now mostly kept locked. Unfortunately, the city limits have stretched uncomfortably close, and in this age of destruction, very little is held sacred. However, according to the needs of the time, the dormant *shakti* can be re-awakened. Nothing is lost, neither created nor un-created. It is. Only the form changes, the expression changes.

tapasya

Chapter 20

Hairakhan

ॐ

Nagendra Haraya Trilochanaya,
Basmanga Ragaya Maheswaraya,
Nithyaya Shudhaya Digambaraya,
Tasmai Nakaraya Namah Shivaya.

– *Shiva Panchakshara Stotram*

Salutations to Lord Shiva
Adorned with the king of snakes
One with three eyes
Smeared with sacred ash
The Lord Supreme
The Eternal One
Purity personified
Whose raiment is the directions themselves

Best known of all the places associated with Babaji is Hairakhan (variously spelled Hadiakhan, Haidakhan, Hariakhan) from where he became known as Hairakhandi Babaji. While Babaji had visited this area previously, when he stayed here for a prolonged time and became a familiar figure, he was referred to by this name. At the cave at the base of the peak of Kumaon Kailash, Manmunindra Mahavatar Hairakhandi Babaji, as he is known, had done severe *tapasya.* Here, many sages and saints had done *tapasya* before that, too. While he is referred to with relation to this village, he is believed to be a *rishi,* connected with Sri Kripacharya and Sri

Ashwasthama, both among the *sapt chiranjeevis* who are ever-existent.

The village itself took its name from the *harada* tree. Harada (haritaki) is one of the ingredients of *triphala*, the other two being *amla* (amlaki) and *behada* (bibhitaki). The etymology of Hairakhan is associated with Lord Shiva. In Sanskrit, Shiva-ji is known as Haritaki or Harhar from where the *harada* plant, abundantly found here, takes it's name.

Hairakhan village is at the base of the Kumaon Kailash peak, which is one of the *up-peeths* of Kailash and is a sacred place of *siddhas.* It is one of the eternal abodes of Lord Shiva. There are sacred rivers that flow here. The *siddha peeths* of Mahadevi Bhagwati Jagdamba are on all the major peaks around, including Surya Devi, Sitla Devi and Siddheshwari *shaktipeeth.* The *sapt rishi ashram* faces the Kumaon Kailash peak. Bhagwati Parvati's *sthan,* in *gupt* or hidden form, is situated in front of the Kailash peak.

At the base of the sacred Kumaon Kailash, the days spent at Hairakhan were of eternal *darshan.* Sri Gorakh Babaji lit his *dhuna* beside the Gautumi Ganga in front of the *gufa* or cave on the evening of Kartik Purnima, when we reached there. He returned to it at intervals maintaining an *akhand dhuna* while we were there. It is through the *dhuna* that *rishis* and *siddhas* reveal the eternal truths. The *dhuna* is the embodiment of *samadhi* and connects the adept to the cosmic energy that vibrates through all manifestation. It is the source of *yogic* knowledge. Through the *dhuna,* the *yogagni* is lit. The *dhuna* is the eternal witness through which spiritual wisdom is revealed to mankind, just as the *Vedas* are the witness of manifestation in all its aspects of creation, preservation and dissolution.

We walked with Sri Gorakh Babaji along the river and through the mountains, as we witnessed in reverence and worship, the lighting of 11 sacred *dhunas.* The journey to Kumaon Kailash, like other journeys to *siddha sthans,* began with the lighting of the *akhand dhuna* Sri Gorakh Babaji maintained during our time beside the sacred cave.

The *siddhas* can be awakened with a call. It is a call rarely heard. Even in deepest *samadhi*, or in any realm they can be alerted. When the call of Kailash is heard, the *siddhas* respond spontaneously. It was this call that I heard reverberating through the Kumaon Kailash *kshetra* in subtle form. I heard it again, as I have heard it in the past, at other blessed times, through the embodied voice and words of Sri Gorakh Babaji, whom I accompanied on this and other sacred *yatras.*

In retrospect, I cannot recall how many days were spent there, absorbed in the timeless space of Hairakhandi Babaji's grace. In the evenings, we would sit and eat the *prasad* cooked in a sanctified *chula* with wood from the nearby forests. We drank the sweet waters from the *naula,* pure and energising. We were deeply aware of being connected to the source of eternal blessings. It was a divine space I was already acutely aware of, and familiar with. At all *siddha sthans* where I have spent time, I have been keenly aware of the depth of experience and revelation. Nowhere have I been more aware of the living presence of Hairakhandi Babaji than at *Siddhashram,* Sitlakhet and in the Kumaon Kailash *kshetra.* At gross levels, almost nothing marks his presence at either. The sacred energy of *siddhas* and *siddha sthans* remain undisturbed despite the external changes in form, circumstances and events.

During our wanderings, Sri Gorakh Babaji talked to the nearby villagers and to those living in the vicinity – the school master, the postman, the tea-shop owner. He sent *prasad* to the school nearby. We entered the homes and temples at which we were invited. We waded across the river, crossing and re-crossing it at several places as we walked along it. An old man told us stories heard from his father and other village elders. He spoke of the many spontaneous miracles around Hairakhandi Babaji, how on occasion he would be in *dhyana* at the *gufa* while he was simultaneously seen on the peak of Kailash by others.

Where the old Kali temple stands on the peak above the current Dak Bungalow, Hairakhandi Babaji would sometimes sit on his way down from Kailash to the village. In front **to his** temple, Sri Gorakh Babaji had done *anusthan* in **1989** . His *trishul* and *chimta* stand in silent protection of the *dhuna.*

On another smaller peak above the river is the Bhagwan Sri Dattatreya *mandir* and *sant-kutir* established by Sri Mahant Godavari Giri-ji of the *Juna Akhada,* disciple of Thanapati Atmananda Giri-ji. I met him at Nandiban Ashram, Parel Gaon, Tank Road in Mumbai several weeks later, when Sri Gorakh Babaji visited him there. I heard again other stories connected with the village of Hairakhan, the Kumaon Kailash *kshetra* and the many *mahatmas* associated with it.

Over the weeks that followed I was keenly aware that I had met yet another great saint, renewed another timeless spiritual connection. On Hanuman Jayanti, I visited Godavari Giri-ji's *ashram* again. I stood outside for many hours in meditation while he remained alone within, absorbed in worship at his *dhuna* in the Dattatreya *mandir.* I met Sri Mahant-ji physically for mere moments. It was an almost wordless meeting. He asked, *"Gorakh kahan hain?"* (Where is Gorakh?)

When I mentioned to Sri Gorakh Babaji that I had been to Nandiban, he said, *"Dattatreya ne bula liya."* (You heeded the call of Dattatreya.)

I have since met Godavari Giri-j several times. His greeting remains the same, "Where is Gorakh?"

Within the *gufa* at Hairakhan, Sri Gorakh Babaji spent several hours in *dhyana samadhi.* The *gufa* itself transformed into a dimension of other spaces. I witnessed the endless dimensions of space that exist within the confines of a physical space. I recognised the *yogic margs* that lead from this sacred cave and the limitless subtle realms of form and formless. I saw the path that leads to Kumaon Kailash which I later climbed. I was graced with *darshan* of Manasarovar Kailash itself as I walked within the sacred spaces of Kumaon Kailash. I knew that Kumaon Kailash is related to Kailash, the ultimate *Siddhashram.* I also learnt of the many *yogic margs* between and

Sri Mahant Godavari Giri-ji

Sri Gorakh Babaji at Manasarovar-Kailash in Tibet

in divine spaces. I saw another path but I was not sure where it led. I was told later that it leads to Haridwar. On other occasions, at Haridwar, I have been deeply aware that the other dimensions are connected within the blink of an eye between life and death.

Time and again, I have returned to the Vashishtha *gufa* beyond Rishikesh and sought the wisdom and understanding that Maharishi Vashishtha and Mata Arundhati had taken birth to reveal to mankind. The *Yoga Vashishtha* contains the Supreme Truth that Maharishi Vashishtha reminded Lord Rama about when he had taken the form of man. This Truth is known through the grace of Mata Saraswati, the embodiment of wisdom and knowledge, the *Shakti* of Lord Brahma, the Creator.

Later, at Pushkar in Rajasthan, I offered my deepest respects at the solitary Brahma *mandir.* It is near the ancient Brahma Sarovar where *srishti* or creation began with the *yagya.* Mata Saraswati manifested herself as the Gayatri while remaining absorbed in *samadhi* at a nearby hilltop where a temple now stands dedicated to her. I climbed the hill to pay my respects to Sri Saraswati, through whose grace this knowledge is revealed and expressed.

At Hairakhan, through the grace of Hairakhandi Babaji, this and other sacred knowledge revealed itself as *darshan.*

CHAPTER 21

Kumaon Kailash Siddha Kshetra

ॐ

Bando Gurupad Kanj Kripa Sindhu Nara Rupa Hari
Mahamohatam Punj Jasu Bachan Ravi Karni Kar
—Guru Vandana from Ramayana

Praise be to the Divine Lotus Feet of the Ocean of Mercy who manifests to remove the darkness of Ignorance through Divine Light

The Himalayas, mighty abode of the gods, *tapasya sthal* of the great *rishi-munis,* is the fountainhead of spiritual knowledge and wisdom. There are many caves and *siddha sthans* at which Manmunindra Hairakhandi Babaji has sat in *dhyana* or meditation, which have been his *tapasya sthal,* where he had performed *yagyas,* built Shiva *mandirs* or lived in *kutias* or dwelling places.

Kumaon Kailash, like Manasarovar Kailash in Tibet has a natural boundary formed by rivers. At the base of the peak, opposite the village of Hairakhan, is the Gautami Ganga river, locally called Gola. At the cave here many sages have meditated in the past. The Gautami Ganga river which flows in this region is so called because of Maharishi Gautam, who had done *tapasya* in this region, along with other rishis. Maharishi Gautam is believed to have sought the Ganga through deep *tapasya.*

Neelgiri Parvat is near the Trayambakeshwar *jyotirlingam,*

close to Nashik in Maharashtra, where the Kumbha is held every 12 years. This is another well known *tapasya sthal* of Maharishi Gautam. Here too, the river Godavari is known as Gautumi Ganga.

Gautam *rishi's ashram* is in front of Kumaon Kailash. The river, Gautumi Ganga flows about 3 kms below this peak. It is said that the Kumaon Katyuri and Chand *rajas*, during their *bhraman* or travels would camp in a flat ground below the peak. The *shakti* here is a *dhuna*, with *chimta, trishul* and *siddha astras* or divine weapons like *dhanush-baan*. There is no temple here, it remains in its natural state, with trees around. It is perceived as an *ashram* of the *sapt rishis* and is a *siddha sthan*. Locals come here on a pilgrimage during *Navaratri* and other festivals.

It is believed that when Lord Shiva sits at Kumaon Kailash, the *rishi-munis* sit here. In ancient times, it is said that it was covered by snow. Because there are no roads here, the vibrations remain undisturbed and *tapaswi yogis*, among them Hairakhandi Babaji, have stayed here in every age, maintaining the intense vibrations of *sadhana* and *tapasya*.

All around Kumaon Kailash are Barhai Devi Jagdamba or *adi shaktipeeths* where the Devi is worshipped. The series of peaks directly connected with Kumaon Kailash are:

- Dev Guru Brihashpati, close by.
- Ahead of this is the Gabori Gufa at Paharpani
- Pashan Devi or the peak of Naina Devi at Nainital
- Nanda Devi or the peak of Almora
- Devi Dhura in Champavat district
- Bandevi or Bandurga near Jalna and Lamgarha
- Dunagiri at Dwarahat near Ranikhet
- Purnagiri at Tanakpur

This region is believed to be inhabited by Ashwasthama. Sri Gorakshanath is believed to be ever present here. He is invoked through *siddha dhuna* worship. Bhagwan Parsuram, among the *Dasavatar* of Lord Vishnu, son of *sapt rishi* Jamdagini and Mata Renuka, is also said to have done *tapasya* in the Kumaon Kailash region.

During the festival of *Shivaratri*, pilgrims come from the villages surrounding Kumaon Kailash to pay homage here. There are three main paths to reach Kumaon Kailash, which connects it to several villages.

Ranibag, where many great sages including *chiranjeevi* Markanday have done *tapasya*, is also at the foothills of Kumaon Kailash. It is described in the *Manas Khand* of the *Skanda Purana*. One path goes from Ranibag via Jamrani and heads left towards the peak. Here there are a couple of villages, including the sacred Jatashankari and the *siddha dhuna* of Gorakshanath en route, where *anushthan* or sacred worship continues to be performed.

Another route from Ranibag heads right, along the river, Gautami Ganga. A path leads to the village of Hairakhan and onto the *gufa* or cave at the base of the peak. There are nine crossings through rivers on this sacred pilgrimage. In front of this cave, there is an ancient Shiva *mandir* and a *peepal* tree which is regarded as a *siddha bat vriksh*.

The third route to the Kumaon Kailash peak is from the Siddheshwar side. There are several roads which lead here from all four directions.

In earlier times, when the pilgrimage to Kailash-Manasrovar was entirely on foot, a well-known route taken by *yogis* and *sant-mahatmas* was from Haldwani-Ranibag through Vijaypur and Hairakhan village, below Devguru Peak. From here the trail was to Nai Gaon and Paharpani village. Thereafter the route was through Sahar Phatak, Nagdeva to Jhankarsain and onto Jageshwar. From here the pilgrimage route was to Haat Kalika *mandir* and to Patal Bhuvaneshwar cave. Thereafter, the road was through Rameshwaram to Pithoragarh and Dharchula. Beyond Dharchula is the route currently used by pilgrims who go on the Kailash *yatra*, supreme among pilgrimages.

On the sacred journey to Kumaon Kailash *siddha kshetra,* I was compelled to remember that total control of our senses and all our emotions is imperative. Without *tapasya* which allows us to overcome our physical limitations and mental modifications, and without surrendering our *ahankar* or ego, we cannot hope to see the divine reality that otherwise remains veiled by *avidya* or ignorance. The Truth is known by piercing the veil of *maya.* He who recognises the divine *lila* or play as it is, recognises the unchanging eternal Self.

To be graced to recognise the divine requires perfect *dharana* or concentration, awareness in walking the razor's edge and total detachment while remaining within the field of action. At Hairakhan, I learnt yet again that the doorway to *siddhalok* is guarded ferociously. One must walk with faith, completely fearless, totally surrendered to the Supreme, without allowing the body, mind and senses to be engaged.

Chapter 22

Devguru Brihashpati

ॐ

Devanam cha Rishinam cha Gurum kaanchan
Sannibhaam buddhi bhutam Trilokesham tam namaami Brihaspatim.

-Guru Stotram

Pranam to Brihashpati, the Guru of the rishis and the gods, precious one, who rules the three worlds with wisdom

Devguru Brihashpati is the *tapasya sthal* of the *guru* of the *devas,* and it is believed that all the gods and goddesses along with Indra, the ruler of the celestial regions, come to visit their *guru* who is ever-existent here along with Tara Devi, his eternal consort. There is an ancient *gufa* below the peak of Devguru, which is a *siddha sthal.* Many known and unknown *siddhas,* including Hairakhandi Babaji, have done *tapasya* here. The *sapt rishis,* too, are believed to have done *tapasya* here.

It is said that Bhishma Pitamah, then known as Devabrata, also learnt *dhanur vidya* or the art and skill of warfare here with the guidance of his mother, the holy Ganga. When Ganga-ji had come to earth in human form, to be the wife of Maharaja Santanu, she bore eight sons, seven of whom she immersed into the Ganga. They were the *Ashth Vasus,* born as mortals to fulfil a curse received by Narada Muni. Only Bhishma Pitamah had to live in the world and play a role, and leave his body at will, when his work was done. It is believed that it was by the grace of Devguru Brihashpati that Ganga-ji had taught the young lad before he was given to his father, Raja Santanu. Later Bhishma Pitamah was guided by Parsurama, among the *Dasavatar* of Lord Vishnu, and also a *chiranjeevi.*

The great warriors of the *Mahabharat*, *yogis* Kripacharya, Dronacharya, Ashwasthama are believed to be present here. Ashwasthama's father is Dronacharya whose father is Maharshi Bharadwaj whose father is Devguru Brihashpati. Another of Devguru Brihashpati's sons is Kacch, who, at the request of Lord Indra, had done *seva* and *tapasya* for 500 years at the *ashram* of Sukracharya to learn *Sanjeevani Vidya* or the secret sacred science of immortality by which life can be breathed into a corpse.

While mortal man is fascinated by the notion of immortality, it is mistakenly associated with the body. Paradoxically, only he who can give up the body, like one changes clothes, realises the immortal Self. *Sanjeevani Vidya, parakaya pravesh* and other sacred knowledge is revealed through divine intervention.

According to old indications, ahead of the peak of Devguru Brihashpati, 9 miles along the trail by foot is Devi Dhura. Saalmali Parvat is 11 miles distant from the peak. In another direction, 11 miles away is Siddheshwar Gautam's *ashram.* Kumaon Kailash is 16 miles from this peak. From near the Gabori *gufa* at Paharpani, the peak is visible at a distance of 7 miles. Amidst these various peaks, Devguru Brihashpati is visible from the many sacred places around. This is the very source of eternal light.

There is a *dhuna* here to mark the presence of this *siddha sthan.* The *dhuna* is the *nirakar swarup* or attributeless form of the Infinite. There are no temples. One km below is a sacred *gufa*, in which many *yogis* have done *tapasya.* Mahavatar Hairakhandi Babaji had stayed here on several occasions and had done *tapasya* here. Because of the strong vibrations in this and other *siddha sthans,* only *purna yogis* or advanced *yogis* and adepts are able to do *tapasya* in these sacred places. Even adepts will prepare themselves before they go to places like this.

It is well known in the *sadhu samaj,* that one must have *yogyata* or fitness to practice specific *sadhana. Tapaswi yogis* hold their *tapasya sthans* as supremely sacred. In an age which seeks to commercialise spirituality, and individual cults have become increasingly fashionable, it must be remembered that *tapasya* has nothing to do with preaching or gathering congregations. Neither *gufas,* nor *siddhas,* nor *devas* will accept one who is not fully prepared. In seeking sacrosanct and esoteric knowledge, one must heed the warnings of the great saints with regard to spiritual practices, sacred teachings and places of sacred worship.

CHAPTER 23

Kailash Darshan

ॐ

Akashaye Tarukalingam
Patalaye Batukeshwaram
Mrityulokaye Mahakalam
Sarva lingam Namastute

—*Shloka/Prayer*

In space Tarukalingam is worshipped
In the nether regions, Batukeshwaram is adored
In Mrityulok or the world of mortal man, Mahakal reigns supreme
Praise be to the all-pervading One in all His glory

The sacred Kailash is revealed through the eternal realms of *darshan.* It's manifestation can be known and enjoyed through physical dimensions, when the *atman* is connected to *Paramatman* and does not identify with the individual body-mind *samskaras,* but is able to transcend the *panch tattwas* and witness, in perfect harmony, the play of manifestation through the three *gunas.*

Impossible to express, define, describe, Kailash is beyond the enigma of pure existence. All theories, known and unknown, all thought, all action, all being is limited in relation to the infinite dimensions of Kailash. While Kailash can be reached through physical co-ordinates, it is not confined or limited by it, and can manifest anywhere, anytime. *Darshan* of Kailash is in the innermost essence of being and the spark ignited remains an *akhand diya* or eternal flame.

Kailash is known as the abode of Lord Shiva. He who seeks *darshan* of Lord Shiva inevitably pays obeisance at Kailash and at all the sacred places associated with Him. The manifest energy of Lord Shiva is everywhere in existence, but more pronounced in particular sacred places which have a direct link because of the *tapasya* and worship which continue to be done there by *rishis, siddhas* and *yogis,* in gross and subtle planes of existence.

The journey to Kumaon Kailash was altogether beyond expression and definition. To write about it, I spent months circumambulating it through *Karma Yoga.* The necessary purification through *tapasya* enables the meditative state through which divine energies are realised. By that alone can we express the images that are beyond thought, expression, form. *Karma Yoga* combined with *Raja Yoga* and *Gyan Yoga* brings the ineffable joy of *Bhakti Yoga,* which is the expression of Higher Truth.

Early one morning we set off from Hairakhan along the river bed of the Gautumi Ganga, climbing vertically up the slope. En route we stopped only to witness Sri Gorakh Babaji light *dhunas.* By afternoon, tired and bone-weary, everyone fell back and found themselves unable to complete the climb. I continued to follow Babaji with determined resolve, through pathless paths, my tired limbs shocked by the burning thorns that seared the skin. When the body has undertaken great penance, one rises above the dimensions of the body. When the senses are controlled and the lower mind of thought is perfectly still, only *sankalpa* for *darshan* remains. One no longer retains ego-identification. Then the *Shakti* or Energy we know is of the Universe, limitless. It was this unbound energy that allowed me to reach the peak of Kumaon Kailash with the smaller twin peak of Devi in front of it.

Babaji had gone ahead and had already gathered wood to light the *dhuna* under the open skies in the *havana kund* before the shelterless temple dedicated to Lord Shiva. Here the *lingam,* with *trishul, chimta* and Nandi in resolute protection, were all open to the directions.

Babaji had carried water from the river at the base of the peak in his *kamandal.* With this, we bathed the *devatas* before offering worship here. Thereafter, we offered water for *snan* of Devi, sitting atop her peak in isolated splendour, shelterless, unadorned, in austere penance. We offered a handful of flowers and heartfelt worship before we offered *ahutis* to *Agni* through *Swaha.* The flames leapt up in primeval delight. The large bells pealed in unison as they were rung to signify the end of the offering.

Here, in the remote Himalayas, with no-one else offering supplication, Bhawani Shankar and Mahadeva, heard the prayers offered, and *darshan* here was of both *nirakar,* attributeless and *shakar,* with form. It was the most unhurried and perfect *darshan* I have known. It opened the path for *darshan* at the other *up*-Kailash, *jyotirlingas, shaktipeeths* and elsewhere I have since offered worship.

In this remote corner of the Kumaon Himalayas, there was not another human being for miles in all directions. Yet, at the moment of *darshan,* Surya Narayana Himself hid behind the clouds which suddenly enveloped the peak of Kailash from all directions. I realised that the sanctity of it must be maintained even from the very directions.

Babaji, whose *kripa* I have been acutely aware of, has often intervened to help me receive the blessings of all whose *darshan* I have sought. He remains witness to the *darshan* at Kumaon Kailash, and the fulfilment of a promise.

Stepping out of the clouds, it was a clear sunlit late afternoon. We hurried downhill to where the others were waiting. They were fast asleep from the exhaustion of the climb. We all continued downhill, keen to reach the *gufa* at Hairakhan near which we were staying, before the twilight turned to night.

Exhausted, we prepared and cooked the only meal of the

day on a wood fire. Several others staying nearby had gathered. Everyone was given *prasad.* In the silence of the still moonlit night, sleep itself was an awakening.

Earlier, my *yatra* to Manasarovar Kailash was only completed when I went to Ganga Sagar where the mighty Ganga meets the ocean in the Bay of Bengal. Now, in the familiar gentle hills of Kumaon, the fullness of the pilgrimage to Kailash Manasarovar in Tibet was experienced again. Hereafter, the *siddha shaktipeeths* I visited revealed themselves in *darshan.* The *yoga marg* to Kailash and the eternal form of Lord Shiva was glimpsed again, and yet again.

This world of appearance is His *maya.* When He chooses to grace us, He reveals Himself in His manifold *Maya.* When we are graced to witness His *Shakti* that veils Him, we know the One in Formless Form.

ॐ Gauri-Shankaraya Namaha
ॐ Hrim Namah Shivaya

CHAPTER 24

Jatashankari

ॐ

Gange Har! Yamune Har! Narmade Har!
Gauri Pate Har Uma Pate Har Parvati Pate Har!
Jatashankari Har Har Mahadeva Har!

–*Sadhu Bani (oral tradition of sanyasins)*

Hail to Ganga, Yamuna, Narmada!
Hail to the Lord of Gauri-Uma-Parvati!
Hail to Jatashankari, Hail Ye Mahadeva!

From Hairakhan to Jatashankari, we walked beside the river, crossing and re-crossing it several times as we did the *parikrama* of Kumaon Kailash. The day before, two young men from Jatashankari village had come to the village of Hairakhan. As Sri Gorakh Babaji sat talking to those around, he chanced to talk to both of them. They agreed to accompany us to Surya Devi. Babaji suddenly decided we would instead go to Kumaon Kailash via Jata Shankari.

As arranged, they arrived early in the morning and we set out after having tea and *rotis* made of *mudgua,* a local black-ish wheat, tasty and nutritious, which was sent by another villager from across the river, where we had visited earlier.

It was an idyllic day of long trekking in the Himalayas – a familiar pastime. There were now six of us. Every time the sun got unbearably hot and we began to tire, wading through the Gautami Ganga rejuvenated us. At several places along the way familiar to Babaji, at the *sangam* or conjuction of two streams, at the base of particular *siddha sthans*, in the front of a cave, we would stop to gather wood as Babaji lit a *dhuna*, before we walked on. It was a wondrous day of awareness of being in the sacred Himalayas, of the energy of the Gautami Ganga and of Kailash. This divine energy is a living reality known by *siddhas* and *yogis* who have done *sadhana* in these remote areas, hidden from curious onlookers. It is revealed through *kripa*.

In the early evening, we stopped at a villager's hut beside the river in the wild unpopulated areas surrounding Kumaon Kailash. We had tea before beginning the hike uphill to the village of Jatashankari. Our next stop was at the home of one of the young men. Here several village elders, and the local *pujari* of the small temple at Jatashankari, gathered for Sri Gorakh Babaji's spontanous *satsangha*. Soon, along with the *pujari*, we were walking towards the temple where we offered our respects. Beyond that, the tumbling waters cascaded through the rocks. I finally had *darshan* of Jatashankari.

The descent of the Ganga to Earth is re-told through a well-known legend. When *Maharaja* Sagar had undertaken the *Ashwamedha yagya*, the horse being used for the *yagya* was stolen by Lord Indra in an attempt to prevent the completion of the *yagya*. Lord Indra had hidden the horse in Kapil Muni's *ashram*. When the horse was found, they reacted from the mistaken premise that Kapil Muni had stolen the horse. *Maharaja* Sagar's sons disturbed the *samadhi* of Kapil Muni and earned his wrath and his curse. All *Maharaja* Sagar's sons were instantly destroyed. Plea for clemency was met by Kapil Muni explaining that the Ganga would have to be sought for their salvation. Accordingly, at Tapovan Kailash above Gaumukh, *Raja* Bhagirath, great grand-son of *Maharaja* Sagar, had done *tapasya* to appease Lord Brahma.

Pleased by Bhagirathi's *tapasya*, Lord Brahma consented to the descent of Ganga. However, he suggested that Lord Shiva be sought first, because if Ganga manifested, the earth would not be able bear the energy of the sacred river. At Kailash

Manasarovar in Tibet, *Raja* Bhagirathi had done *tapasya* to appease Lord Shiva. It is through Jatashankari's matted locks that the great Ganga is held, to stem her unrestrained flow as she descends to Earth. At Kailash-Manasarovar, the Ganga is believed to be in subtle form, descending to *Patal* or the underworlds before emerging at Gaumukh in the familiar form in which she is revered by millions.

Bhajamana Rama Charana Sukh Dayi
Rama Charana Sukh Dayi, Shiva Charana Sukh Dayi
Jin charana se nikasi surasarir
Shankar Jata samayi
Jatashankari naam paro hai
Tribhuvan taran aiy

(Praise Lord Rama, incarnation of Lord Vishnu by meditating at His feet. From His feet have emerged the surasarir or Devanadi Ganga, sacred river of divine origin. It descends through the matted locks of Bhagwan Shankar and is so called Jata Shankari. The Ganga has come to purify the three worlds of Bhur, Bhuvah, Swah, which refer to the gross mortal plane, the intermediary regions of the ancestors and the celestial realms.)

The region of Kumaon Kailash is dry, seemingly bereft of any source of water. There is a place where it is said that there was a small pool of water resembling Manasarovar. Mata Parvati is symbolised by the slightly smaller peak in front of Kumaon Kailash. The Gautumi Ganga has its source lower down where it emerges from amidst the rocks, seemingly as though it descends through the matted locks of Jatashankari. This entire region is naturally carved in replica of Kailash Manasarovar and the many legends associated with the eternal *rishis.* This sacred region, where Devguru Brihashpati, *guru* of the *devas,* is believed to dwell, and where *rishis* and *siddhas* from nameless ages have done *tapasya,* is the manifest energy of revelation.

The sweet waters as they emerge here from the rocks are *amrit* indeed – the very nectar of immortality which rejuvenates and purifies. And the old legends of Ganga-ji's descent to Earth comes to life here. The *rishis*, seers of mantra, eternal witnesses of the divine play, through whom *samadhi* is revealed to mankind, continue to reveal these eternal Truths.

At Jatashankari, we stayed in a simple village hut in this remote, poor village, which has neither electricity nor any facilities, far from any motorable road. We were looked after with the greatest warmth and hospitality. Two nights spent here was a lifetime of old connections. In the evenings we kept the chill of approaching winter at bay with a wood fire lit in a large metal bowl filled with earth.

In the early morning before we set off for Kailash, I bathed in the cowshed with water carried from some distance away. This second visit to Kumaon Kailash, there were some ten of us who sat around the sacred fire at Kailash. This time, *darshan* was a memory hidden behind clouds, beyond the senses. There was time to see the peaks around and be aware of the physical reality of this sacred region. I was able to appreciate the subtle essence that compels us to return unknowingly to that which usually remains hidden.

On our return from the peak of Kailash, we were served one of the best meals I have tasted. I had already heard that it was a favourite meal of Hairakhandi Babaji: *sushumna ka saag* which is made from the thorny *bicchu buti, mudgua ka roti* and *bhatt ki dal,* a local lentil.

The next day, in the dark of pre-dawn night, I accompanied Babaji to the temple below Jatashankari to pay our respects in farewell. At dawn we started our long hike back till Jamnani from where we hitched a ride on a truck to reach civilisation and hire a jeep to Haldwani. The two villagers from Jatashankari who had accompanied us from Hairakhan, returned with us to Haldwani, reluctant to part with Babaji.

Again and again, I have realised that reaching the higher Himalayas is supremely ennobling. These isolated areas where time stands still are hidden spaces of sacred energy. Pilgrim and trekker alike are aware of a deep sense of joy, fulfilment and peace when they are blessed to enjoy the remote Himalayas, where people are compelled to surrender to the powers that be. Those that belong here are often completely unaware that the vibrations here are so different. They are usually spontaneously simpler, warmer people with a higher sense of community and an innate goodness, until external influences create conflicts.

When returning from these sacred places of high energy, the journey back is jarring unless we are conscious of having transcended our everyday gross consciousness and equally aware of the return to it. The screeching horns and traffic jam at Haldwani was the usual rude awakening to city realities, to conveniences, amenities and the intangible price we pay for it.

As Babaji had remarked after a Kailash-Manasarovar *yatra* when this was strikingly apparent, "They went into the *Satya Yuga* and returned into the *Kali Yuga.*" And that, in sum, is what it is all about. An ascent to a higher consciousness allows us to enjoy the divine realms. The descent to our gross, material awareness is congruent with loss of our sense of Higher Self. We connect easily with the Self when our vision is purified through *nishkama karmayoga* or detached action, *tapasya* or austerities, *sadhana* or spiritual discipline and practice, *bhakti or dev*otion and *kripa* or grace.

CHAPTER 25

Gyangunj

ॐ

Om Pragyanam Brahman

—Mahavakya, Aitreya Upanishad, Rig Veda

Supreme Wisdom is Brahman

Darshan of *siddha sthans* is possible for *siddhas, siddha sadhaks* and those graced by an adept. It is difficult to comprehend the language of *yogis*, more difficult to express it. Having known the joy of the ineffable, it is inevitable that we seek to share it.

Sri Gorakh Babaji has said:

"Many speak of *Siddhashram*. Of *Gyangunj*. As a mystical place which exists but remains unknown, except to those who have been graced to know it. Manasarovar-Kailash is *Siddhashram*. Elsewhere, is a reflection of this *Siddhashram*, and is connected to that very source.

"Kailash is attained through *tapasya*. The *rishis* have kept alive the tradition of *tapasya* from the beginning of time. Brahma, Vishnu and Mahesh are the fountainhead of *tapasya*. They are the *anadi* or eternal *Guru* through whom all wisdom is revealed. This is the divine source. *Mata* Parvati or Bhawani, Jagdamba, Uma is the *Devi* of *tapasya* and the essence of all *Devis*, worshipped at *siddha shaktipeeths*. To understand the concept of divinity, to manifest that divinity within, *tapasya* is the form and the path.

"Uttarakhand Himalayas of Bharat are the land of *tapasya* of the *rishi-munis.* The vibrations of *tapasya* are still alive here. It is these vibrations which reverberate in the hearts of seekers, why pilgrims tread these paths in a trance of worship, why humanity comes to these hallowed grounds where he stands face to face with himself.

"At Kailash, the mountains, the rivers, the very stones themselves are the form behind which that subtle essence is hidden, and can be perceived through *kripa.* This is *darshan.* The veil of *maya* or illusion and delusion causes us to perceive with our senses, instead of connecting to the *atman,* limitless, without barriers. Here is *Gyangunj.*

"*Gyan* is related to Bhagwan Shankar. It cannot be seen by the eyes. *Darshan* of this is only possible for *rishis, siddhas, yogis* and *mahatmas. Gyangunj* cannot be seen as *atman* cannot be seen, *siddhas* cannot be seen as *atman* cannot be seen. To know *Gyan-Kailash,* we have to enter *Gyangunj.*

"The *sapt* Kailash associated with Manasarovar Kailash are *up*-Kailash or subsidiaries of Kailash itself. Experience of it is not possible without being *suksham.* The Truth cannot be known through Untruth. *Yoga* purifies the body, mind, thoughts, actions through which the subtle becomes perceivable. Through our speech, action and behaviour we reflect this purity.

"*Divya ashrams,* and *siddha sthans* can only be visited in purified form. People often seek *Gyangunj.* There are many references to it in current populist 'spiritual' literature. People have indicated its whereabouts. Only *tapaswis* can know it, only through *tapasya* can it be known, *tapasya darshan* is the only way. Even *sanyas* is through *tapasya,* otherwise it is mere form. People on the *bhog marg* talk about visiting *Gyangunj.* It cannot be visited without *Gyan.* He who has *atman-gyan* can have *darshan* of *siddhas* and *siddha sthans.* Else, going to the same place at the same time, the experience will be purely physical and mental not *yogic* and spiritual.

"When Damayanti was roaming in the forest, alone and bereft, she wandered into a *siddhashram* and spoke to the *siddhas* there. She was not focused on her own woes. Because of her higher nature, she was graced by *darshan*. She received the blessings of the *siddhas* whereby she knew her time of trial would pass, and through it she was able to perceive the Higher Reality. The *siddhashram* itself vanished. And so of all *siddha sthans*. They are there and not there. We can perceive it, not in imagination, but it manifests itself for a particular time. To know it is *darshan*.

"*Dhuna pani, siddho ke bani*
Jahan mile lakkar, vahin mast fakkar.

(The sacred fire pit and water, the wisdom of the *siddha*. Where there is wood, the saint without possessions remains in bliss).

"The *dhuni* is regarded as the *Mata* – it protects and nurtures the *yogi* as does the mother. *Akhand dhunis* of *siddhas* are the continual flow of energy connected to the very source. All *samskaras* are burnt in this sacred fire.

"*Dhuna darshan* is an integral aspect of *sadhus*. In the *akhadas* in the tradition of *sadhu-sanyasins*, the *dhuna* is revered as specially significant. All *sadhus* cannot maintain a *dhuna* at an *akhada* – only one who is recognised as having the *adhikaar* or merit to maintain a *dhuna* will do so.

"There are different kinds of *dhunas*. *Siddha dhunas* are maintained with extreme sanctity. *Panch agni tapasya* is done through the medium of the *dhuna*.

"Manmunindra Hairakhandeshwar Acharya and Sombari Babaji's *dhunas* are held in the highest respect and reverence as places of worship. The *dhunas* of *siddha-sadhus* are found in all corners of Bharat. Matsyendranth-ji and Gorakhnath-ji's *dhunas* are found in many places through the length and breadth of our motherland. In Uttarakhand, most villages maintain the tradition of *dhunas. Grihasthas* or householders maintain *tapasya* here in the *rishi parampara* or tradition maintained through the *rishis.* The *rajas* or kings were aware of the power of the *dhuna* and many forts were built with the blessings of a *dhuna.*

"The *dhuni* is the very basis of understanding and transcending the *panch tattwas* of earth, water, fire, air and ether. Through the *dhuna,* direct knowledge is transmitted, the eternal Truth is revealed. This is *gyan. Atman gyan* is not about theoretical and academic knowledge. It is known through direct experience.

"The *chimta, trishul, khadga* and other sacred symbols associated with the *dhuna* have deep spiritual significance revealed through *sadhana.* It is important to realise that a *divya astra* remains in *gupt* or sacred non-revealed form, in non-physical dimensions. What is seen is a mere symbol, the physical aspect of a manifest energy. In this physical form it is a *shastra* or weapon, albeit with the potential of immeasurable power. The infinite power of a divine *astra* is of dimensions beyond human understanding, vision and thought. The power of a divine *astra* is harnessed through *sankalpa* or determined will of the higher realms of the *siddha patal.*

"At the *dhuna,* what remains after the *ahuti* or offerings to the sacred fire, is *vibhuti* or the sacred ash – One without a second. The sacred ash is powerful beyond measure. For *sadhus* and *yogis, vibhuti* is the mother: *"Vibhuti mai jahan pai tahi lagayi".*

"*Vibhuti* is deeply connected with *mantra sadhana. Sadhu-sant sanyasins* use *vibhuti* in sacred worship. Here it is a symbol of *vairagya* and *tyaga,* or renunciation and asceticism. For a *sadhu* who is one-pointed in the practice of *sadhana,* it generates *vairagya* and *tyaga,* the true wealth of a *sadhu.* It represents the infinite power that emanates from worship at the *dhuni.* It is what remains of the life offerings of one who has devoted his very being to the One, having burnt all else in the sacrificial fire. It is the essence of the wisdom gained. And eventually, it is also the *shakti* or power of the Infinite that is bestowed in divine grace through the *dhuni* in the form of the purest of the pure – the *vibhuti.*

"At a *dhuna, gyan-yagya* is performed. The Self is the offering. In physical terms, the *vibhuti* remains. In spiritual terms, *gyan* or wisdom is attained. *Vibhuti* is this very *gyan.*

"Bhagwan Shankar is depicted covered with sacred ash. Here, the *vibhuti* that covers Lord Shiva is *Prakriti* or *Shakti.* All creation emerges from Him and dissolves within Him, and the *vibhuti* is the eternal aspect of it. In *yogic* terms, *vibhuti* is the *alakh niranjan*, the *Advaita* aspect – when all else is reduced to ashes, what remains is the non-duality of *vibhuti* alone. Sadashiva is All.

"Bhagwan Shankar is the spiritual and *yogic* fountainhead of *vibhuti shakti*, or the power that is inherent in *vibhuti. Vibhuti darshan* is a matter of the *siddha patal.* The hidden sacred *shakti* of *vibhuti* has been delegated by Lord Shiva to the *siddhas*, who through *sadhana* have realised the *shakti* of *vibhuti.* In *siddhalok*, through the *vibhuti mantra*, creation itself can be generated. The manifold powers or *shakti* associated with *siddhas* are because of their ability to create and cause to manifest.

"*Atman darshan* is knowing this *vibhuti*, which is the cause of the universe and the cause of its dissolution. With *kaam, krodh, lobh, moha and ahankar* reduced to ashes, it is possible to experience the state of *siddhattwa.* This is *gyan* through which one is graced with *darshan* of *Gyangunj* and *Siddhashram.*"

The continued living presence of Sri Hairakhandi Babaji, of the *rishis* and *siddhas,* is known through *sadhana* and *tapasya* which prepares us to receive *kripa,* which itself is immeasurably subtle. Within the mighty Himalayas this energy is reflected everywhere. With purified vision, we have *darshan* of this. Then we begin to learn how Lord Shiva is worshipped.

I have known Lord Shiva's *bhaktas.* They are without fear. Yet Lord Shiva is the fear of the fearless. And they fear Him even when they have crossed the threshold of fearlessness. They remain alert and vigilant even when they have surrendered all action. Knowing it is Shiva-ji who does everything, knowing He is the cause and He is the end, knowing there is nothing but Lord Shiva, each step they walk is measured by the *prana* or breath that is taken to remember His name.

ॐ

Glossary

The meanings given are not a literal translation, but are with reference to the spiritual context and implication within the current framework. An accurate translation of Sanskrit terms is probably impossible in many cases. Sanskrit is the language in which the Vedas and all literature pertaining to the Sanatan Dharma, the eternal Truth, have been expressed. It is concise, precise and the vibrations of the words themselves impact the consciousness. To express it in English is at best, a mere interpretation, and therefore subjective and given to error.

acharya : accomplished teacher

adi siddha : *adi* is the origin, *adi siddha* refers to Lord Shiva

advaita : non-duality (of consciousness), Absolute Unity

agni : fire, refers to the energy of fire, spiritual fire

agni samadhi : yogic process of dissolving the body with the energy of the fire element, *agni*

aham brahmasmi : I am Brahman. It is a *Mahavakya* or Great Saying from the Vedas. *(Brihadaranyaka Upanishad).*

ahankar : ego or I-consciousness, in context of *manas, buddhi, chitta, ahankar*

akhand : continual, unbroken

amrit : nectar, ambrosia, elixir of life

anahata nada : uncreated sound, cosmic vibration

antardhyan : without body/ego consciousness, also used in context of disappearance from the physical realm

anushthan : observance, worship according to prescribed tradition, generally for a specific time period

aparadh : offence

ashram : hermitage

ashtha-dha prakriti : five *tatwas* or elements + three *gunas* or attributes, the essence of manifestation

ashtha-siddhi	: the eight *siddhis*
atman	: transcendental Self, Consciousness
atman gyan	: knowledge of Self
atman gyani	: one who has perfect Self knowledge
avadhut	: one who is totally free. Sri Gorakshanath describes in detail the state of an *avadhut* in *Siddha Siddhanta Paddhati*
Avatar	: Divine Incarnation
avtarit	: incarnate
banj	: oak
Bhagwan	: God, godhead
bhagawat lila	: divine play
bhajan	: devotional song
bhandaar	: storehouse, treasure
bhandara	: feast
bhandari	: one who maintains the storehouse/treasure
bhasma	: *vibhuti*, sacred ash
bhav	: state of mind, intense feeling, uplifted emotion
bhraman	: wandering
birya, virya	: sexual energy, semen
brahmacharya	: celibacy
brahma drishti	: divine vision, inner vision
Brahman	: Absolute Reality, Supreme Existence-Consciousness
brus	: rhododendron
buggal	: ceremonial stone fight on *Raksha Bandhan* in Devi Dhura, Kumaon
charitra	: character
chida akasha	: space of inner consciousness
chimta	: tongs
chir	: pine
chiranjeevi	: immortal
chita bhasma lepo	: applying the ash from cremation grounds as a sacred ritual

coolie : labourer

dakshina : offering

darshan : 'seeing' with inner vision or Brahma *drishti*

Darshana : The *Shat (Shad) Darshana* or six schools of philosophy:

Nyaya founded by Maharishi Gautama

Vaiseshika by Maharishi Kanada

Samkhya by Maharishi Kapila Muni

Yoga by Maharishi Patanjali

Purva Mimamsa by Maharishi Jaimini

Uttara Mimamsa or Vedanta by Maharishi Vyasa

devadar : cedrus deodara

deva : god, divine power

devaloka : celestial realms

dhanush-baan : bow and arrow

dharma : that which sustains the natural state, the universal law of nature

dharma yudh : war to maintain the universal law of nature

dharamshala : refuge

dhoti : single cloth draped on lower body

dhuna : sacred fire pit

dhyan, dhyana : meditative absorption

doli : palanquin

dosh, dosha : fault, blemish

dvaita : duality

gaddi : chair, position

ghanta : bell

gobar : cowdung

grihastha ashram : householder and the duties and obligations thereof

gufa : cave

gunas : attributes

gupt gufa : sacred hidden cave

guru diksha	:	initiation into spiritual life by a preceptor
guru maharaj	:	preceptor
gyan	:	knowledge, wisdom
haldu	:	Haldina, also known as *Kadamba*
havana	:	sacred fire offering
him samadhi	:	taking *samadhi* in the snow
ishtha deva	:	personal deity
itihaas	:	history
jagrat	:	awakened
jal samadhi	:	taking *samadhi* in water, or dissolving the body into the element of water
Janamashtami	:	Lord Krishna's birthday
japa	:	recitation of *mantra*
juneau	:	sacred thread
jyoti	:	light, divine light
kaal	:	time
kaam	:	desire
kalash	:	pot, vessel, container
Kali yuga	:	age of spiritual decline, current age
kalpa	:	an eon equal to one day in the life of Brahma the Creator consisting of 1,000 *yugas*. Also see *yuga*
kamandal	:	sacred water pot
kaphal	:	myrica esculenta; a tree with tasty, cherry-sized off-white to reddish fruits
kapre	:	cloth, clothes, also referring to saffron cloth symbolising renunciation
karma	:	activity subject to universal law of causation, of action and reaction
karma-tyagi, karma-vyaparit	:	one who is free of karma, i.e. performs only detached ego-less selfless action
kaya (parakaya) pravesh	:	entering the body of another
khadga	:	sword

kirtan	:	devotional music
kosha	:	sheath: physical, subtle and causal *annamaya kosha*: gross physical body *pranamaya kosha*: etheric body of life energy *manomaya kosha*: subtle sheath of the *manas* or mind connected to the five senses *vigyanmaya kosha*: wisdom body or discriminating higher mind *ananadamaya kosha*: causal body of bliss
kripa	:	grace, blessing, compassion, mercy
kriya	:	an action, specific purificatory technique or practice with the aim of attaining and remaining in higher states of consciousness/being
kund	:	large vessel, pit, pond
kutia	:	dwelling place
lakshan	:	indications
lavang, elaichi, supari	:	cloves, cardamom, beetelnut
lila	:	divine play
lingam	:	symbol of the formless, attributeless Brahman, indivisible, all-pervading, eternal, auspicious, ever-pure, immortal essence of this vast universe
loka	:	realm, sphere, planes of existence including physical, subtle, causal
lota	:	metal vessel for water
maharathi	:	outstanding warrior and great charioteer
mahatma	:	great soul
mahavatar	:	divine incarnation
mahayug	:	see *yuga*
manas putra	:	mind born sons of Brahma, the Creator
mandir	:	temple
mantra	:	the sound form of reality, having the power to bring into being the reality it represents.
manvantar	:	see *yuga*
marg darshak	:	one who shows the way, teacher

maya	:	cosmic illusion
Mimamsa	:	system of enquiry, reflection and interpretation. Among the six orthodox philosophical systems *Purvamimamsa*: based on ritual traditions rooted in the *Vedas* and the *Brahmanas* *Uttaramimamsa: Vedanta.*
mitti	:	earth, mud
Mrit Sanjeevani Vidya	:	study and knowledge of the science of immortality
mrityuloka	:	the world of mortal beings
mula	:	main, chief,
murti	:	idol
nada	:	primal sound *Ahata nada*: consciously produced sound, music *Anahata nada*: uncreated sound, cosmic vibration of being
naam japa	:	recitation of divine name
nag (naga)	:	snake, a kind of astral being
Naga sanyasin	:	particular class of sanyasins who protect and defend the faith. As part of their austere renunciation they may be completely naked, on particular occasions, or perpetually
Navaratri	:	festival of nine nights dedicated to Devi
nishkama karmayoga	:	action with detachment to the fruit of action
nirakar swarup	:	formless form, without attributes, all-pervading
niranjan	:	eternal, beyond attributes
paap	:	sin, fault, demerit
palki	:	palanquin
parikrama	:	circumambulation in worship
panch agni	:	five sacred fires, where four fires are kindled in each of the cardinal directions, and the Sun is the fifth
panch tattwas	:	five elements of *bhumi* or earth, *jal* or water, *agni* or fire, *vayu* or air and *akash* or ether

Pandavas : five sons of *Raja* Pandu: Yudhishthir, Bhima, Arjun, Nakul & Sahadeva

paori : axe

param tapaswi : supreme ascetic, adept

Paramhamsa : Literally Supreme Swan, one with the highest spiritual realisation. A *hamsa* or swan can separate milk from water, and symbolises one who can discriminate between the Real and unreal, pure and impure and enjoin himself with the pure, perfect. For the *Paramhamsa*, all is Divine, he embodies divinity

peepal : ficus religiosa, a type of fig tree

prakar : different kinds

Prakriti : nature, feminine principle

the basis of matter composed of the three *gunas* of *Tamas* or ignorance, inertia; *Rajas* or passion, action; and *Sattwa* or purity. Also see *purush*

pralaya : cosmic dissolution

prana : life energy, the vital energy of breath

prasad : offering to a deity, which is then taken by devotees, with the inherent blessings of the deity

prateek : symbol

puja : worship

pujari : priest, one who performs worship

Purana : encyclopaedic texts containing the essence of the *Vedas.* Written to popularise the philosohy of the *Vedas* and foster devotion to God through myths, legends and stories of *mahapurusha* or evolved beings. They also chronicle great historical events.

Purush, Purusha : the Self, which pervades the universe. The *Purusha Sukta* of *Rig Veda* praises Him whose mind is the moon, eyes are the sun, and breath the wind.

rishis : seers of the *Vedas* who realise the truth directly and reveal it *sadhak* : spiritual aspirant

sadhana : spiritual practice

sadhu : *sanyasin*, one who has renounced

sahaj (sahaja) : natural, effortless, spontaneous

samadhi : state of unitive consciousness

Samkhya : one of the *Shat Darshana* or six schools of philosophy.

samparna yogiraj : perfect *yogi*

sampradaya : sect

samskara : the subconscious impressions left by each action which leads to renewed psycho-mental activity

samshan ghat : cremation grounds

sanatan : everlasting, eternal

sangam : confluence

sangrakshak : protector

sanyas : renunciation

sanyas diksha : initiation into *sanyas* or the adoption of renunciation

sanyasin : renunciate

Sarvam Khalvidam Brahman : all is Brahman

satsangha : literally, in the company of truth. The practice of meeting saints, sages, adepts, and their disciples, in whose company the ultimate Reality can be more readily experienced

shakar : with form

Shakti : spiritual power; the divine cosmic energy which projects, maintains and dissolves the universe. the energy/power of manifestation, action

also the consort of the male expression of the divine, especially with relation to Lord Shiva.

shakti diksha : awakening or transference of spiritual energy. In current age, this is mostly symbolic. It is a rare phenomenon of the manifestation of divine grace through the medium of a *satguru* or enlightened master to an *adhikari* or *shishya* of exceptional merit.

shaktipeeth	:	places of Shakti or energy where Devi is worshipped. These are associated with Sati taking *agni samadhi* at her father Daksha Prajapati's *yagya.* The places where different parts of her body fell as Lord Shiva carried her corpse, are *shaktipeeths*
shankha	:	conch shell
shastra	:	scriptures, also the knowledge thereof
shishya	:	disciple, student
Shivaratri	:	great night of Shiva, on the fourteenth day of the dark half of the lunar month of Phalguna (Feb/March) when Lord Shiva is specially worshipped
shraddha	:	abiding faith, pre-requisite for the spiritual path
siddha	:	Self-realised adept or perfected being
Smritis	:	remembered knowledge. Codes of ethics, those of Manu, Yajnavalkya and Parasara are considered authoratative
Srutis	:	revealed knowledge ie *Vedas.*
suksham sharir	:	subtle body
swadhyaya	:	Introspective study of Self and scriptural texts, specially that pertaining to the Self
swargaloka	:	celestial realms
swarup	:	natural or true form, essential nature, an appearance or form that is revelatory in nature
swayambhu	:	self-manifested
tap, tapasya	:	austerities, asceticism, spiritual discipline which leads to enhanced vitality
tapasya kaal	:	time of maintainng austerities
tatwa darshan	:	philosophy and wisdom pertaining to *tattwas* or the elements of earth, water, fire, air & ether
teerth sthan	:	places of pilgrimage
teerth yatra	:	pilgrimage
tejas	:	radiance, the energy of fire
thana	:	lock-up
tol	:	measure

tope : cap

trishul : sacred trident

Upanishads : ancient Scriptures of Vedanta

upasana : literally sitting near, meditation, worship

urdhva-retas bramhacharya: an adept in celibacy whose semen flows upwards

veda vakya : Truths of the *Vedas* which are the basis of contemplation for spiritual wisdom

vibhuti : sacred ash from the sacrificial fire

videha, videhi : one who is not limited by the body, can exist without the body

vidhwan : knowledge holder, also knower of Self

vidya : esoteric knowledge, particular paths or doctrines of study

vishwas : trust, faith, belief

yagya, yagna : fire sacrifice

yatra : journey

Yoga : Absolute Union, science of Self-realisaion, also Patanjali's philosophy of *Yoga*

yogic prakriya : techniques and practice of *yoga*

yogi : one who is perfected in *yoga or* an advanced practitioner with a high state of spiritual insight

yogini : *yogi* (female)

yogmaya, yogamaya : conscious potency, the created world illusion

yuga : age or cycle, a prescribed world era

Satya (or Krita): The Golden Age of Truth

Treta: Silver Age associated with Ramayana

Dwapar : Bronze Age ended with Mahabharat

Kali Yuga : Current Iron Age of spiritual decline

The descent from Satya to Kali marks a deterioration of Dharma.

All four and the transition periods taken together make a *mahayug.*

71 *mahayugs* make a *manvantar*

14 *manvantars* make a *kalpa,* a cosmic age